James Hogg

THE GROWTH OF A WRITER

James Hogg

THE GROWTH OF A WRITER

David Groves

1988
SCOTTISH ACADEMIC PRESS
EDINBURGH

First published in Great Britain, 1988,
by Scottish Academic Press Limited,
33 Montgomery Street, Edinburgh EH7 5JX.

ISBN 0 7073 0455 8

British Library Cataloguing in Publication Data

Groves, David
    James Hogg: the growth of a writer.
    1. Poetry in English. Hogg, James, 1770-1835 — Critical studies
    I. Title
    821'.7

    ISBN 0-7073-0455-8

Scottish Academic Press
acknowledges subsidy from the Scottish Arts Council
towards the publication of this volume.

Typeset at Oxford University Computing Service.
Printed by Lindsay & Co Ltd, Edinburgh.

CONTENTS

ACKNOWLEDGEMENTS

Quotations from original manuscripts have been made with the kind permission of the Alexander Turnbull Library of Wellington, New Zealand, and of the Trustees of the National Library of Scotland. A fellowship from the Social Sciences and Humanities Research Council of Canada enabled me to live in Scotland while preparing this book. I am also indebted to Douglas and Wilma Mack for their patient understanding and helpful comments.

Chapter One

THE ARTIST AS A YOUNG MAN

READERS of *The Scots Magazine* in 1794 found a poem called 'The Mistakes of a Night' in the October issue. This anonymous piece was the first by James Hogg to appear in print. Written in the Scots vernacular tradition of Allan Ramsay and Robert Burns, it tells the story of a youth who mistakenly seduces his girlfriend's mother:

> TAK my advice, ye airy lads,   Take
> That gang to see the lasses,   go
> Keep weel your mind, for troth, the jads
> Tell ilka thing that passes.   every
> Anither thing I wad advise,
> To gang on moon-light weather:
> A friend o' mine, he was sae wise,   so
> He kiss't his lass's mither
> Ae Friday's Night.[1]

The sense of rapid movement and the dark, mysterious landscape are characteristic of Hogg's writing:

> Awa' gaed Geordie hip and thigh,   Away went
> Out-o'er the muir to Maggy:
> The night was neither warm nor dry,
> The road was rough an' haggy:
> . . . .
> Then aff into the barn they hye,   off
> To spend the night in courtin';
> The widow's heart did sing for joy,
> To think o' her good fortune,
> That Friday's night.

Later the widow becomes pregnant, Geordie is dragged before the church elders to learn his 'grand mistake', and, to his regret, he is

1

forced to marry her. The ending is abrupt, harsh, and almost tragic.

Geordie's bride is the first of several loving, encouraging mother-figures portrayed by James Hogg; it is worth remembering that eight years later he described *Hamlet* as 'one of the best plays of my favourite author'.[2] The main feature of Hogg's first poem is ambiguity, which appears in the mixture of comedy with tragic undertones, in the poet's uneasy balance between arousing his reader's passions and conforming to conventional morality, and above all in the young hero's acutely ambivalent response to the widow. Like most of the poems, stories, and novels written by James Hogg, 'The Mistakes of a Night' follows a descending path from initial confidence into confusion, ambiguity, and chaos. The shotgun marriage at the end of this poem is probably as unsatisfying to the reader as it is to Geordie, but in his later, better works Hogg learns to forge a more thoughtful resolution by confronting the implications of chaos more fully.

Very few first poems are as lively, readable, and deeply suggestive, as 'The Mistakes of a Night'. The author's pride must have been dampened, however, when the editor added a footnote to explain,

> We are disposed to give the above a place to encourage a young poet. We hope he will improve, for which end we advise him to be at more pains to make his rhymes answer, and to attend more to grammatical accuracy.

Hogg was to hear echoes of this kind of snobbish, sterile criticism, to the end of his life.

James Hogg was born in Ettrick Forest, a rolling, remote, sheep-farming area in the south of Scotland. His parents were tenant farmers, and his mother, in her spare time, was practically 'a living miscellany of old songs'[3] from Scotland's past. At school young Jamie hated the teacher for his

> thin shrivell'd cheek,
> And grey eye of intolerant tyranny!
> His wig of dirty brown that scantly reach'd
> Half way unto his ear: all frizzled round
> With fringe of thin grey hair. His coat threadbare,

2

Long-back'd and shapeless, and the pocket-holes
A weary width between.[4]

For many years Hogg could dream 'Of ample, hideous, and most dire revenge / For youthful degradation', until slowly his hatred for the teacher softened into a more ambivalent attitude, one which sees good and bad in the same character. Hogg conceded in his old age that the teacher had had 'A face of brass, to hide a heart of love'. Even when whipping the students the teacher would turn away 'That none might see him wipe the falling tear / From off the wither'd cheek'. Both the teacher, and James Hogg in his adult years, were fundamentally divided about questions of authority or power.

Fortunately the future poet was soon liberated from the schoolroom. His parents lost their money and were 'turned out of doors without a farthing in the world'.[5] James was taken from school and placed as a cowherd on a neighbour's farm. He continued to work as a cowherd, general farm labourer, and shepherd, until his late thirties. During his teens he used his free time to learn the fiddle, which he 'prosecuted with such diligence', a neighbour recalls, 'that he frequently spent whole nights' practising, despite the warnings of his parents, who worried that 'too much indulgence . . . would cause a levity in the after part of life, and in the mean time to a neglect of his master's business'.[6] Hogg received only six months of schooling, but he taught himself to read by memorising the Psalms. At seventeen he was trying to read Allan Ramsay's *Gentle Shepherd*. His master's wife

took some notice of me, and frequently gave me books to read while tending the ewes; these were chiefly theological. The only one, that I remember any thing of, is 'Bishop Burnet's Theory of the Conflagration of the Earth'. Happy it was for me that I did not understand it! for the little of it that I did understand had nearly overturned my brain altogether. All the day I was pondering on the grand millennium, and the reign of the saints; and all the night dreaming of new heavens and a new earth — the stars in horror, and the world in flames! Mrs. Laidlaw also gave me sometimes the newspapers, which I pored on with great earnestness — beginning at the date, and reading straight on, through

3

advertisements . . . and every thing; and, after all, was often no wiser than when I began.[7]

James Hogg continued to read widely all his life. His early writings show an appreciation for Fielding, Pope, Swift, Oliver Goldsmith, and Burns, as well as for renaissance drama and classical poetry in translation. The pastoral poems of Virgil (translated by Dryden) were an obvious influence, and as early as twenty-two Hogg was reading and attempting to imitate 'Dryden's Virgil'.[8] In his 'Letters on Poetry: by the Ettrick Shepherd', written in 1805, he advises young writers to immerse themselves in literary tradition, and to 'improve your understanding, and correct your taste,' by making a habit of 'reading one hour' before 'writing two'.[9]

At twenty, the shepherd was 'fair, ruddy, with big blue eyes', and

> blessed with strong health and the most exuberant animal spirits. . . . His head was covered with . . . light brown hair, which he usually wore coiled up under his hat. . . . [On entering church] he used to raise his right hand to his hair to assist a shake of his head, when his long hair fell over his loins, and every female eye was upon him, as with a light step he ascended the stair to the gallery.[10]

James Hogg was usually happy, healthy, at home in his rural community, and able to integrate aspects of life which more puritanical minds would see as polar opposites. He often recalled, in later years, his adventures as 'an admirer of the other sex':[11]

> I remember of a girl once falling asleep below my plaid, on a wet day, when, in the depth of her slumber, she fell a talking, and, addressing me as another man, revealed a secret of her own which she ought not to have done. . . . When I apprised her afterwards of what she had told me, she cried bitterly, and said, 'she had tauld me a great big lee, but she couldna help it'.[12]

In his thirty-odd years as a shepherd James Hogg often spent whole days or weeks alone on the hills with only the sheep and his sheep-dog for company. Sirrah, his first dog, was notorious for his

> outrageous ear for music. He never heard music, but he drew towards it; and he never drew towards it, but he joined in it with all his vigour. Many a good psalm, song, and tune, was he the cause of being spoiled; for when he set fairly to, at which he was not slack, the voices of all his coadjutors had no chance with his. It was customary with the worthy old farmer with whom I resided, to perform family worship evening and morning; and before he began, it was always necessary to drive Sirrah to the fields, and close the door. If this was at any time forgot or neglected, the moment that the psalm was raised, he joined with all his zeal, and at such a rate, that he drowned the voices of the family before three lines could be sung. Nothing farther could be done till Sirrah was expelled. But then! when he got to the peat-stack knowe before the door, especially if he got a blow in going out, he *did* give his powers of voice full scope . . . , and even at that distance he was a hard match for us all.[13]

Sirrah was succeeded by his son Hector, who was also endowed with a genius for music. It happened that at one period James Hogg was chosen to lead the church in singing. Unluckily Hector was waiting outside the church window, and, seeing his master standing at the front, and hearing his voice, the dog began to croon

> with such overpowering vehemence, that he and I seldom got any to join in the music but our two selves. The shepherds hid their heads, and laid them down on the backs of the seats rowed in their plaids, and the lasses looked down to the ground and laughed till their faces grew red. I despised to stick the tune, and therefore was obliged to carry on . . . ; but I was, time after time, so completely put out of all countenance with the brute, that I was obliged to give up my office in disgust.[14]

Hogg's love for animals and for nature accounts for many of his attitudes as a writer. But unlike a few of his contemporaries,

James Hogg never idealised nature and never lost sight of its potential for destruction. One of his best early stories tells of a snowstorm which began innocently with 'small thin flakes that seemed to hover and reel in the air as if uncertain whether to go upward or downward'.[15] By the following day several shepherds and thousands of sheep had perished:

> When we came to the ground where these sheep should have been, there was not one of them above the snow. Here and there, at a great distance from each other, we could perceive the head or horns of one appearing, and these were easily got out, but when we had collected these few we could find no more. They had been lying all abroad in a scattered state when the storm came on, and were covered over just as they had been lying.[16]

At twenty-four, Jamie was summoned to court as a witness in a trial for poaching. A friend informs us that the shepherd 'either evaded or refused to give direct answers', until

> at length seeing there was no alternative, he reluctantly complied, but at the same time told his persecutors, that he would soon find a way to expose their ignorance and sacreligious conduct to the world; and accordingly he immediately set about writing his *Scots Gentleman.*

This comic drama, which has not survived, was apparently 'so replete with blunt but natural answers, that it never fails to excite the most lively burst of laughter, when read to an Ettrick audience'.[17] His conduct at the trial for poaching reveals two important characteristics of James Hogg: a preference for natural emotion over strict literal truth, and for community over authority. Thirty-six years later the Ettrick Shepherd would live up to his threat by writing 'The Poachers', a bitter satire against the game laws.

During his twenties James Hogg was often shoeless, wore tattered clothes beneath a large shepherd's plaid, and slept in the hayloft of a barn. He wrote many songs, poems, and dramas, which were read or performed at local dances, weddings, or fairs. His second appearance in print was the patriotic song 'Donald

M'Donald', written on the eve of a threatened invasion of Britain by Napoleon.

Hogg apparently carried this song to Edinburgh while driving sheep to the city market in 1800. Once the sheep were sold he

> called on his old Ettrick friend Mr. Mercer then editor of the North British Magazine. . . . Mr. Mercer being a friend to genius, asked the young shepherd to dine with him in a celebrated chop-house in the Fleshmarket Close, and a very happy night was the result to both.

The shepherd sang his 'Donald M'Donald' at the table. Within a few weeks 'Edition followed edition', and soon 'the whole country rang with the patriotic strain'.[18]

Although hardly a great poem, 'Donald M'Donald' is an effective combination of diplomacy, politics, and high spirits. It tries to reunite a divided Scotland, and reconcile Scotland to England, by presenting former disputes in a humourous light. Highlanders had been Jacobites in the past, Donald maintains, merely because of their innate 'tenderness' and charity:

> What tho' we befriendit young CHARLEY,   Prince Charles Stuart
>   To tell it I dinna think shame,
> Poor lad he came to us but barely,
>   And reckoned our mountains his hame;   home
> 'Tis true that our reason forbade us,
>   But tenderness carry'd the day,
> Had GEORDY come friendless amang us,   King George II
>   Wi' him we had a' gane away.[19]

The poet creates a feeling of community through sarcasm, humour, and incantation:

> If BONAPARTE land at Fort William,
>   Auld Europe nae langer sal grane,   shall groan
> I laugh when I think how we'll gall him,
>   Wi' bullet, wi' steel, an' wi' stane.
> Wi' rocks o' the Nevis an' Gairy,
>   We'll rattle him aff frae our shore;
> Or lull him asleep in a cairney,
>   An' sing him *Lochaber no more*.

7

'Donald M'Donald' was a great success, for it sold well, and Napoleon was frightened away. At a banquet of the Edinburgh cavalry attended by Walter Scott, the song was apparently

> joined in with such glee that all the Mess got up joined hands and danced round the table and added Scott 'I joined the ring too and danced as well as I could and there were four chaps all of the Clan Donachie who got so elevated that they got up upon the top of the table and danced a highland reel'.[20]

In 1803 the poet would perform his song for friends during one of his Highland tours:

> We met a most kind welcome from [the host], whom we found in the midst of a great room-full of ladies, with only one or two young gentlemen, of whom he complained that they would not drink any . . . . The drinking was renewed on our entering, . . . and we soon became remarkably merry, screwed up the fiddles, and raised a considerable dance. It was here that I ventured to sing my song of Donald M'Donald . . . . It was so highly applauded here that I sang it very often during the rest of my journey.[21]

Hogg again drove sheep to Edinburgh in November 1801, where he arranged for a printing of his *Scottish Pastorals, Poems, Songs, &c.* at his own expense. The seven pieces in *Scottish Pastorals* certainly lack polish, yet they also reveal keen observation, freshness, and originality. Following Allan Ramsay and other Scottish and English poets of the eighteenth century, Hogg has used classical pastoral conventions and structure to depict life in his own time and place. The first poem is 'Geordie Fa's Dirge', an amazing work which mourns the death of a Scottish gipsy:

> BAITH auld and young come join wi' me;
> Come greet as if ye'd lost a plea;   cry; lawsuit
> Come shake your head , an' whinge, an' claw,
> An' murn the death of Geordie Fa.
> Auld 'onest, hearty, jocun' carle!
> Without a grane he left the warl':   groan; world
> Death in a twinklin' quite bereft us
> O' a' our joy, whan Geordie left us.[22]

8

A popular fiddler, sportsman, and raconteur, Geordie Fa was evidently a mainstay of social cohesion in his rural community:

> Wi' beggars, sodgers, merchants, taylors,
> Ev'n wi' the warst o' broken sailors,
> He wad hae crackit hale forenoons,   conversed
> An' played them half a score o' tunes.
> Wi' a philosopher or poet,
> The way they took, was fond to know it;
> An' wi' the rich he kept decorum;
> But now he's dead, an' waes me for him.

'Geordie Fa's Dirge' is James Hogg's experiment in the formal genre of pastoral elegy, complete with a pleasure-loving gipsy as a rather unconventional replacement for the nature-god of traditional pastoral. In a tone deliberately light and rustic, it laments the passage of time and the loss of an older Scotland which allegedly had maintained a better balance of rich and poor, young and old, and nature and society.

The second of the *Scottish Pastorals* is 'Dusty; or, Watie an' Geordie's Review of Politics'. On a Scottish hillside, two shepherds argue the merits of William Pitt's government. Geordie, a Presbyterian Whig, sides with the radicals and French revolutionaries, while Watie supports Pitt and demands that his friend

> Shew me the signs o' Britain's ruin,
> An' wha's the cause o' her undoin'.

The radical Geordie then complains of the decline of religion and growth of high taxes, adultery, and war, adding that

> Fo'ks een are open'd now, they see   Folks' eyes
> The French design them liberty;
> By' makin' laws which fo'ks admire,
> They've won mair than by sword an' fire.

Watie's response to these charges is the first of Hogg's many attacks on the Enlightenment assumption of a disembodied and purely rational intellect: not only have Geordie's 'cursed notions'

9

made his cheeks thin and his eyes yellow, says Watie, but they have also

> banish'd frae your mind content,
> The greatest bliss that heav'n has lent.

However, we soon find that Geordie's real grievance is against William Pitt's new tax on dogs, which has resulted in the death of his sheep-dog Dusty. Unwilling to pay the tax of five shillings a year, Geordie allowed the soldiers to take Dusty and hang him:

> He had some prospect o' the deed,
> For back he drew, and wadna lead,
> His looks to me, I'll ne'er forget them,
> Nae doubt he lookit for protection;
> While I, unfeeling as the tree,
> Stood still, an' saw him hung on hie.
> At first he spurr'd, an' fell a bocking,   retching
> Then gollar'd, pisht, and just was choaking: howled
> Deil tak the King, an' burn his crown,   Devil take
> Quoth I, an' ran to cut him down.

When Geordie tried to free Dusty at the last minute, the dying dog bit him 'till the blude did spring'. Geordie jumped back, 'Confus'd an' hurt', and Dusty 'sprawl'd to death' before his eyes. These surprising, daring changes of tone and action indicate a strong dramatic sense and look ahead to the hanging scene in Hogg's *Confessions of a Justified Sinner* twenty-three years later. With its thoughtful use of rhetoric and drama, this poem expresses Hogg's support for Pitt's government, while also conveying an underlying ambivalence which concedes the unfairness of some of Pitt's policies. For all of its roughness, 'Dusty' achieves an evocative combination of past and present, balance and spontaneity, and tragic involvement and comic distance:

> But yet for a' his gruesome dealins',
> He was a dog o' tender feelin's:
> When I lay sick an' like to die,
> He watch'd me wi' a constant eye;
> . . . .
> When saams were sung at any meetin',   Psalms
> He yowl'd, an' thought the fock war greetin'. folk were crying

10

The error of Geordie's radical politics is symbolised, in 'Dusty', by Geordie's betrayal of his dog. Yet the last lines of the poem balance this impression, with Watie admitting that he too has given up a dog to the government soldiers. However much their politics and other intellectual attitudes may separate the two shepherds, they are united by their love of dogs and their relationship to the natural world.

Hogg's first collection also includes his graveyard poem, 'Dialogue in a Country Church-yard'. In this piece a shepherd-poet recalls dreaming of 'a long long journey' to 'A dismal lake'.

> Near to that awful lake I drew,
> Thro' which a passage ne'er was found.

Millions of people, including the dreamer, are trapped on the side of a cliff. One by one they drop into the dark water below. The dreamer feels 'a beam of joy' when he looks up to see 'the FRIEND OF MAN', but this friend turns into a tree and suddenly plunges down into the lake. Next morning the poet learns from another shepherd that Mr Bryden, 'that tender friend, / That rais'd us both when press'd so low', has died. This is the first of many tributes to 'the late worthy Mr Brydon',[23] who, twenty-four years earlier, found a home and employment for the penniless Hogg family. The black lake of despair, then, symbolises two disasters which greatly affected James Hogg in his youth: the death of his first benefactor Mr Bryden, and his own childhood trauma of being taken from home and set to work as a labourer at the age of seven.

The young poet was well aware of the value of educated friends who could direct him in his reading, his writing, and his public career. At thirty-one he ventured to write to Walter Scott:

> I am far from supposing that a person of your discernment.
> d—n it I'll blot out that word 'tis so like flattery. I say I
> don't think you would dismiss a sheperds 'humble cot an'
> hamely fare' as Burn hath it yet though I would be ex-
> tremely proud of the visit yet hang me if I would know what
> to do w'ye.[24]

A few weeks later Scott came to Ettrick, listened to Hogg's mother sing her ballads, and invited Hogg to visit him in

11

Edinburgh. The shepherd paid his sensational return visit just before Christmas in 1803. Although dressed as an 'ordinary herdsman attend[ing] cattle to the market', and with hands stained with tar from a recent sheep-smearing, James Hogg apparently put his feet up on the sofa, 'dined heartily and drank freely, and, by jest, anecdote, and song, afforded plentiful merriment'.[25] In his letter of apology Hogg blamed 'the fumes of the liquors':

> I am afraid that I was at least half seas over the last night I was with you for I cannot for my life remember what passed when it was late. . . . I have the consolation however of remembering that Mrs. Scott kept us company all or most of the time which she certainly would not have done had I been very rude. I remember too of the filial injunction you gave at parting cautioning me against being insnared by the loose women in town. . . . [26]

Throughout his thirties Hogg went on several trips by foot, horse, and boat, to the Highlands, Islands, and other parts of Scotland. His impressions, published in letters in the *Scots Magazine*, indicate an active, fun-loving, observant man, always trying to improve himself by reading, and inclined to self-mockery. They give no hint of the despair he must have felt on being cheated out of ten years' savings by a farmer in Harris. Little is known of his trips to the north of England, but in later years he could remember

> stripping to the waist to wade the Tyne —
> The English Tyne, dark, sluggish, broad, and deep;
> And just when middle-way, there caught mine eye,
> A lamprey of enormous size pursuing me!
> L— what a fright! I bobb'd, I splashed, I flew!
> He had a creditor's keen ominous look,
> I never saw an uglier — but a real one.[27]

Energy, rapid transitions, and metaphors that tie together the human and animal worlds, are hallmarks of the Shepherd's best writing. Even in this passage, with its 'correct', genteel syntax, he

12

maintains an agility, a freedom of mind, which saves him from artificiality.

The *Scottish Pastorals* had not been the commercial success its author had expected. He was now ashamed of his first collection, and he feared that certain political allusions might cause trouble. Meanwhile public taste was pushing him towards a more sentimental, melodramatic, and 'proper' style which would be less challenging socially, and less satisfying to the artist. A correspondent in *The Scots Magazine* in 1807 complained of Hogg's 'total want of Taste', lumping him with other rustic 'versifiers who lard your Miscellany with *Scottish Poetry*', and who, 'Inattentive to common delicacy', seemed to enjoy insulting readers with 'what is gross and offensive', thus besmirching the 'divine art'[28] of poetry. Even Thomas Cunningham, a poet and friend of the Shepherd, advised James Hogg to write safe, sentimental verses which shed the 'sympathetic tear':

> I ha'e a heart, an' sae ha'e ye,
> Owre rife o' sensibility.[29]

Over

Fortunately Hogg never surrendered to foolish suggestions like these, but his next book, *The Mountain Bard*, shows little evidence of his talent for satire, analysis, or provocation. In a revealing letter to Scott, Hogg thanks his friend for his editorial help, admits to 'a failing in being so adverse to all alterations', and adds regretfully that since 'a poet is no judge of his own productions I must just lay my hand on my mouth and my mouth in the dust'.[30]

Despite its delicacy, politeness, and other defects, *The Mountain Bard* indicates the poet's growing awareness of the artistic potential inherent in local legends and traditions. And one of its pieces, 'Robin and Nanny', is a startling exception to the tameness of the volume as a whole. This daring poem was omitted from the first edition, but was quietly slipped in near the back of the 1821 edition. Hogg introduces 'Robin and Nanny' with great caution, explaining beforehand that

> It is exceedingly imperfect; but a natural fondness for the productions of my early years . . . induce[s] me to give it a place. It has not the least resemblance in style to aught I

13

have written since. . . . Those who wish me well will not regret that my style has undergone such a manifest change; for into a worse one it could scarcely have fallen.

After these careful excuses, the poet proceeds to tell a shockingly lively tale of a Highland lass who ends up at an Edinburgh brothel. Mary sets out to walk to the city at the age of eighteen:

> Cauld, that day, came in the winter,
>   Light she tripped adown the dale;
> Dash, a gig came up ahint her,   behind
>   Swifter than the mountain gale.
>
> 'Bonny lassie, ye'll be weary,
>   Will ye mount an' ride wi' me?'
> . . .
>
> Crack the whip came, — snortin', prancin',
>   Down the glen the courser sprang;
> Mary's heart wi' joy was dancin',
>   Baith her lugs wi' pleasure rang.   Both her ears

In the capital Mary finds work as a servant until her mistress fires her in a fit of jealousy. As an older servant piously explains,

> Mistress lang had slyly watched her,
>   Doubtin' sair her 'haviour light,
> An' wi' gentle spark had catched her   youth
>   At the dead hour o' the night.
>
> Straight she turned her aff in anger,
>   Quite owre ruin's fearfu' brink;   over
> Virtue steels her breast nae langer,
>   As she brewed she now maun drink.   must

Luckily Mary's father comes to Edinburgh just in time to save her from a life of prostitution. As he walks towards her Robin hears his daughter begging admission to the brothel:

> 'Let me in', she cried, 'till mornin';
>   Then I'se trouble you nae mair'.
> They within, her mis'ry scornin',
>   Stormed, an' threatened unco sair.   very sorely

14

'A' your whinin's out o' season;
  We hae borne w'ye mony a day;
Had ye listened ought to reason,
  Ye had been a lady gay;

'Might hae in your chariot ridden,
  Clad wi' silks o' ev'ry hue,
Had ye done as ye were bidden: —
  Get ye gone, or ye shall rue'.

'O, I am a helpless creature,
  Let me in, for sair I rue!
Though it shocks my very nature,
  What you bid me I will do'.

The poem ends happily with forgiveness and a return to their
rural community. A much more typical poem in *The Mountain
Bard* is 'Sandy Tod', where Biblical imagery follows a pattern
from creation to apocalypse, with the shepherd being crossed in
love and committing suicide. At times the verse comes alive with
good puns and ironies:

  You ha'e seen, on April mornin',
    Light o' heart, the pretty lamb
  Skippin', dancin', bondage scornin',
    Wander heedless o' its dam?

The poet, like the lamb, has a licence to 'Wander heedless' above
and below the everyday world, yet his social function, in this
poem, now requires that he act as a kind of chaperone, shielding
his comfortable audience from the tragic vision:

  No, my dear, I winna shock ye
  Wi' the bloody scene below.

The critics approved, of course. Their response pointed out the
path Hogg must follow if he wanted to be a success in polite
society. An Oxford reviewer quaintly noted that 'Ease, sweetness,
and unaffected simplicity adorn the pages of this little volume',
from which 'readers of every class will derive unmingled plea-

15

sure'. *The Cabinet, or Monthly Report of Polite Literature* worried about the increase of 'rustic versifiers . . . who, being once praised for rhyming, are little inclined to attend to any thing else', but the *Monthly Review* announced that this 'not inelegant poesy' was a great step forward for Hogg, since its 'diction is visibly more correct, and less at variance with the rules of good taste and propriety'. Another reader might cavil at the 'too circumstantial description of disagreeable objects', yet even so he thought that *The Mountain Bard* would 'steal a tear from every reader of sensibility'.[31]

James Hogg's reaction to this polite praise was to try to get as far away from genteel urban society as he could. *The Mountain Bard* brought him more than two hundred pounds, and another eighty-six pounds came in for a non-fiction book called *The Shepherd's Guide: Being a Practical Treatise on the Diseases of Sheep*. The famous author 'went perfectly mad' with joy and pride, taking his money out of Edinburgh and buying a 'pasture farm, at exactly one half more than it was worth, having been cheated into it by a great rascal'. It seems that the rascal 'meant to rob me of all I had, and which, in the course of one year, he effected by dint of law'. For three years Hogg 'blundered and struggled on' as a farmer, 'giving up all thoughts of poetry or literature of any kind'. At length he was 'run aground' and forced to give his creditors 'all that I had'.[32] Dr James Browne, LL.D., a fervid and long-time antagonist of the Shepherd, gives a less flattering picture of Hogg as 'a fugitive insolvent'[33] hiding from angry creditors.

About this time Hogg also fathered two illegitimate children. In a letter written in 1817 he admits to having 'two very lovely daughters who bear my name the one 11 the other 8 years of age'. 'I have myself stood with a red face', says the proud father, 'on the Stool of Repentance'. His letter explains that the two mothers afterwards married

> men much more respectable in life than ever I was . . . and even with their nearest relations I have never been for a day out of favour. The aunt of one of the young ladies ventured in full assembly of friends to propose marriage to me with her lovely niece. I said I was sure she advised me well but really I could not get time. She said I had had plenty of time

since Candlesmass. 'O yes said I that's very true but then the weather was so wet I could not get through the water' at which they all burst out a laughing, the girl herself among the rest and there was no more of the matter nor was there ever a frown on either side. If you now saw my Keatie at church with her hat and feather and green pelice you would think it the best turn ever I did in my life.[34]

Back in Edinburgh in 1810, James Hogg published *The Forest Minstrel*, a collection of songs, fifty-seven by himself, and twenty-five by other Scottish poets. Though with less success than *The Mountain Bard*, Hogg's contributions to this volume cater to polite taste, and mainly avoid vulgarity, politics, or any challenge to set morality. In general they simply try to arouse basic emotions like fear, pity, love, or laughter. An example is 'Bonny Dundee', where a soldier's seduction of a maiden symbolises the religious hatreds that have divided Scotland in the past:

O, where were the feelin's o' that cruel villain,
Who rifled that blossom, an' left it to die?

One critic found in these lyrics 'a peculiar kind of sublimity' produced by 'the plainness, and even rudeness of the language, contrasting with the loftiness of the thought'.[35] Yet their practical effect is to encase the reader and the poet in an intense subjectivity which ignores present objective realities such as the direction of society, economic change, or social relationships.

The Forest Minstrel invites readers to indulge in amorous phantasies, but to avoid passion by recognising the dangers of sexuality. Even the comic songs, despite their gentle attacks on Edinburgh society, ultimately endorse respectability by asking us to laugh at the folly of physical love. In Hogg's marvellous 'The Drinkin', O; A Sang for the Ladies', the lovesick women of Edinburgh are imagined to chant mournfully,

O WAE to the wearifu' drinkin', O!
That foe to reflection an' thinkin', O!
Our charms are gi'en in vain!
Social conversation's gane!
For the rattlin' o' guns an' the drinkin', O!

17

Similarly, Hogg's 'Doctor Monro' makes fun of a love-sick young man who cries out to his physician,

> DEAR Doctor, be clever, and fling off your beaver;
> Come bleed me, and blister me, do not be slow:
> I'm sick, I'm exhausted, my schemes they are blasted,
> And all driven heels-o'er-head, Doctor Monro.

Whether comic or sentimental, Hogg's songs in *The Forest Minstrel* tell us that love is a dangerous, chaotic experience which undermines human freedom, dignity, and reason.

Just like *The Mountain Bard*, *The Forest Minstrel* contains one poem by Hogg which tries to unsettle the status quo. The song 'How Foolish are Mankind' begins in a vein of innocent philosophical reflection:

> How foolish are mankind, to look for perfection
>   In any poor changeling under the sun!
> By nature, or habit, or want of reflection,
>   To vices or folly we heedlessly run.
> The man who is modest and kind in his nature,
>   And open and cheerful in every degree;
> Who feels for the woes of his own fellow-creature,
>   Though subject to failings, is dear unto me.

At the end of what seems like an innocuous song, however, these abstract ideas are suddenly brought to bear on the political situation of the day:

> Far dearer to me is the thrush or the linnet,
>   ˙ Than any fine bird from a far foreign tree;
> And dearer my lad, with his plaid and blue bonnet,
>   Than all our rich nobles or lords that I see.

The Forest Minstrel was not a great success commercially, in spite of Hogg's obvious attempts to appeal to a middle-class book-buying public. *The Scots Magazine* liked its 'tenderness and pathos' but hinted ominously that certain Scottish poets 'seem ambitious . . . to exclude every trace of refinement, and to outdo even the vulgarity of the lowest vulgar'.[36]

18

Hogg's first writings demonstrate a strong fascination for ambiguity, ambivalence, and chaos. From 'The Mistakes of a Night' to *The Forest Minstrel*, his protagonists typically embark on a descent into a world of confusion which engulfs physical, spiritual, and psychological aspects of human life. The author's ambivalence may be towards a parental figure, teacher, politician, or towards society or the audience, while his main characters are sometimes almost tragically ambivalent, as in 'The Mistakes of a Night' or 'Dusty'. Quite often the obscurity of this lower realm is suggested through liquid images of misty nights, foggy days, a river, alcohol, tears, or a black lake of despair and death. In *The Mountain Bard* and *Forest Minstrel* the reader is usually shielded from chaos, but in Hogg's better pieces a reader can hardly avoid following the protagonist and the author on their descent.

Two poems, 'Donald M'Donald' and 'Geordie Fa's Dirge', might not seem to fit this pattern. However, their vision of community and togetherness represents the second half of what I call Hogg's distinctive personal 'myth' of descent. That myth traces an individual's downward journey into confusion and despair, followed by the essential discovery of human fellowship and finally the return to community and social values. James Hogg has not yet found his pathway from despair to affirmation, but still the two sides of the parabola, descent and return, can be found in his earliest work. The broader vision will emerge in his next project, a weekly magazine with the provocative name of *The Spy*.

Notes

1 *Scots Magazine*, Oct. 1794, p.624; slightly amended.
2 A Shepherd, 'A Journey Through the Highlands and Islands of Scotland, in the Months of July and August 1802', *Scots Magazine*, Dec. 1802, pp. 956-63. Hogg saw a production of *Hamlet* in 1802 with his friend Andrew Mercer of the *North British Magazine*.
3 Hogg, letter to Walter Scott, 30 June (1802), in the National Library of Scotland (hereafter NLS), MS 3874, f. 114.
4 Hogg, 'The Dominie', *Edinburgh Literary Journal*, 26 Mar. 1831, p. 199.
5 Hogg, 'Memoir of the Author's Life', in *Memoir of the Author's Life and Familiar Anecdotes of Sir Walter Scott*, ed. Douglas S. Mack (Edinburgh and London, 1972), p. 4.

6   Anon., 'Biographical Sketches of the Ettrick Shepherd', *Scots Magazine*, Jan. 1805, p. 14.
7   Hogg, 'Memoir', p. 9.
8   Hogg, 'Memoir', p. 82.
9   Hogg, 'Letters on Poetry', II, *Scots Magazine*, Jan. 1806, pp. 17-20.
10 William Laidlaw, quoted by R. Borland, *James Hogg, The Ettrick Shepherd: Memorial Volume* (Selkirk, 1898), pp. 8-9.
11 Hogg, 'Memoir', p. 6.
12 Hogg, 'Aunt Susan', *Fraser's Magazine*, July 1831, pp. 720-26.
13 Hogg, 'Further Anecdotes of the Shepherd's Dog', *Blackwood's Magazine*, Mar. 1818, pp. 621-26.
14 Hogg, 'The Shepherd's Calendar: Class IV; Dogs', *Blackwood's Magazine*, Feb. 1824, pp. 177-83.
15 Hogg, 'Storms', rpt. in *James Hogg: Selected Stories and Sketches*, ed. Douglas S. Mack (Edinburgh, 1982), p. 5.
16 Hogg, 'Storms', p. 13.
17 Z, 'Further Particulars in the Life of James Hogg, the Ettrick Shepherd', *Scots Magazine*, July 1805, p. 503.
18 R. G., 'The Ettrick Shepherd's First Song', *Edinburgh Literary Journal*, 8 May 1830, pp. 275-76.
19 Hogg, *Donald M'Donald: A Favourite New Scots Song* (Edinburgh, 1801); slightly amended. The words and music are reprinted in full in the Appendix to Hogg's *Anecdotes of Sir W. Scott*, ed. Douglas S. Mack (Edinburgh, 1983), pp. 66-67.
20 Hogg, 'Familiar Anecdotes of Sir Walter Scott', in *Memoir of the Author's Life and Familiar Anecdotes of Sir Walter Scott*, p. 119.
21 'Unpublished Letters of James Hogg', *Scottish Review*, July 1888, pp. 37-38.
22 Unless otherwise stated, all quotations of James Hogg's writings are taken from the first published editions, as listed in the Bibliography.
23 Hogg, 'Memoir', pp. 4-5.
24 Letter to Scott, 30 June (1802), NLS 3874, f. 114.
25 John Gibson Lockhart, *Memoirs of the Life of Sir Walter Scott, Bart.*, 7 vols. (Edinburgh and London, 1837), I, 408-09.
26 Letter to Scott, 24 Dec. (1803), NLS 3874, f. 248.
27 Hogg, 'Disagreeables', *Fraser's Magazine*, June 1831, pp. 567-69.
28 An Old Critic, 'On the Art of Writing Poetry in the Scottish Dialect', *Scots Magazine*, June 1807, pp. 412-15.
29 T. M. C., 'To J— H— inclosing the following', *Scots Magazine*, June 1807, p. 448.
30 Letter to Scott, 23 Oct. 1806, quoted in Alan Lang Strout, *The Life and Letters of James Hogg, The Ettrick Shepherd (1770-1825)* (Lubbock, Texas, 1946), p. 34.
31 Anon. revs. in *Oxford Review*, Nov. 1807, p. 541; *Cabinet*, July 1807, p. 333; *Monthly Review*, Aug. 1821, p. 428; and *Scots Magazine*, April 1807, pp. 283, 285.
32 Hogg, 'Memoir', p. 18.

33 An Old Dissector, *The 'Life' of the Ettrick Shepherd Anatomized; in a Series of Strictures on the Autobiography of James Hogg* (Edinburgh, 1832), p. 13.
34 Letter to John Aitken, 20 Dec, 1817, NLS Acc. 8879.
35 Anon. rev., *Scots Magazine*, Aug. 1810, p. 604.
36 Anon. rev., *Scots Magazine*, Aug. 1810, pp. 604, 608.

Chapter Two

HUMBLE GENIUS

THE first number of *The Spy* came out on Saturday, the first of September, 1810. Its fictitious editor, 'Mr Spy', was an ingenious mask which aided James Hogg both in venting his ambivalence towards Edinburgh society, and in working out a mature response to the sentimental, subjective expectations of his genteel audience. Mr Spy introduces himself as 'a bachelor, about sixty years of age', 'a simple old man, who has only left the mountains a few years ago' to settle in the capital. His shifty personality is the cause of Mr Spy's many failures in the past, and a mark of his unusual ability to enter the subjectivity of other human beings:

> I am now become an observer so accurate, that by con-
> templating a person's features minutely, modelling my own
> after the same manner as nearly as possible, and putting my
> body into the same posture which seems most familiar to
> them, I can ascertain the compass of their minds and
> thoughts, to a few items, either on the one side or the other,
> — not precisely what they are thinking of at the time, but
> the way that they would think about any thing.

The innerness of other people, considered as isolated, self-contained entities, is what fascinates Mr Spy. His character will be Hogg's vehicle for exploring, exaggerating, and satirising the self-indulgent, sentimental, *Mountain Bard* outlook demanded by most of his polite readers. Like many authors who hope to appeal to a comfortable upper- and middle-class audience, the Spy will emphasise his sympathetic powers, his capacity for vividly imagining the subjective experience of individuals, while prudently trying to avoid objective social analysis or any hint of questioning the values, direction, or structure of society as a whole.

Quite appropriately Mr Spy concedes that his gift for entering other minds has its disadvantages from a practical point-of-view. In his school-days he 'fell insensibly into a habit of imitating' the teacher, even to 'the same ridiculous loud ha, ha, of a laugh; the same shake in my walk, with my arms set a-kimbo, and my hat a little on one side; and even the same way of spitting, and adjusting my neckcloth; so that the pedant . . . conceived the idea that I mimicked him for sport'. Years later, after training for a preacher, the Spy found to his horror that during his first sermon he wandered absentmindedly from the text and began to assume the absurd mannerisms of one of the old parishioners. Equally disastrous careers as a farmer and poet followed in quick succession.

Even though Mr Spy conforms (in his idiosyncratic manner) to the ruling subjectivism of the age, he departs from conventional genteel expectations in one important way. He admits the priority of physical and economic facts and their powerful influence on the mind. Past failures have repeatedly exploded his subjective pretensions by forcing him to face a bleakly objective world which includes such harsh realities as economic self-interest, the need to keep a job, and the ways of pleasing a teacher, boss, customer, or audience. This darker realm is superbly symbolised when, having arrived in Edinburgh and set himself up as a 'Spy upon the manners, customs, and particular characters of all ranks of people', he follows 'three beautiful young ladies', aping their mannerisms so as to understand their thoughts, and suddenly stumbles into a deep pool of water. The water is 'above my depth, and the shore being a perpendicular wall, I had certainly perished if it had not been for the ladies, the innocent causers of my misfortune'. The women rescue Mr Spy with a silk scarf, then laugh at him and exclaim 'that it would have been as becoming in me to have been looking to my own feet, or thinking upon my grave rather than upon them'. The dark, inescapable pool, surrounded by laughing young women, represents physical reality, the womb, the power of women over men, the chaos of sexuality, and ultimately the grave. Women are both the cause of the Spy's misfortune, and the rescue.

Although an extreme subjectivist by temperament and philosophy, Mr Spy has learned, through his disastrous confrontations with the objective world, to distrust the power and pride of intellect. He assumes that the best way to understand others is not by listening to what they say or think, but by observing physical details such as posture, facial expression, mannerisms, and clothing. Without exception his stories all tend towards reducing human beings (including himself) to the physical or economic. Habitually skeptical of pretensions to objective reason, he often insists that value judgments are only the manifestations of vanity:

> First impressions are always most permanent. This, the inherent principle of self-esteem, will ever secure to us: for when once we have formed an opinion of any thing in our own minds, we have too high a sense of our own judgments again to retract, without the utmost reluctance; even though reason should remonstrate.

His distrust of the intellect accounts for Mr Spy's hatred of Francis Jeffrey, editor of the best-selling *Edinburgh Review*. Jeffrey's supposedly rational, philosophical book-reviews are apparently only expressions of

> the temperature of the weather, his own frame and disposition at the time of reading the works, or the nature of the books which he has been reading immediately before them. .

> For an instance, — we shall suppose this notable reviewer, on a cold day in December, sitting at his desk; the window perhaps facing to the north — his feet smarting with cold, and his hand scarcely able to hold the pen wherewith he marks the delible (take care and do not read damnable) passages; his eagle eye brushing impatiently over the pages —
>
> > *'Then woe to the author, and woe to his cause,*
> > *'When J-----y his weapon indignantly draws'.*

All human beings, even the famous intellectual Francis Jeffrey, are, it seems, limited by their subjectivity and their involvement in physical processes. '[H]ow little dependence', observes Mr Spy, 'ought to be placed upon the discriminating and appreciating powers of any one mind'. For James Hogg, as for Mr Spy, Jeffrey is a prime example of the Anglicised Scot, the man who rejects his own nationality and community traditions under a pretense of objective reason. Jeffrey, that 'envious little scoundrel about this town', apparently cannot even 'endure to hear either man or woman, of this nation, applauded excepting himself and those of his party'. Yet this person has 'set himself up as a principal connoisseur' for a great many of his fellow-countrymen, who abandon their own judgment and 'even consent to be led by the nose'. Although this 'malicious rascal' is only 'a mere vehicle' for Whig politics, he nevertheless entertains 'a presumptuous opinion of [his own] inherent perception, and infallible discernment'. Jeffrey's rationalism is a mask, Hogg implies, for prejudice, self-interest, conformity to English ways, and a tyrannical temperament that seeks to impose uniform standards on everyone. As Hogg wrote elsewhere at this time, concerning Jeffrey,

> So sharp was his lash, when his temper was fired,
> At the breath of his nostrils the authors expired.
> . . .
> For the rich or the poor he car'd never a button;
> But stuck to his party, and ventur'd his mutton.[1]

Hogg's belief was that good criticism should be imaginative rather than just intellectual. He offers his own version of literary criticism in a series entitled 'Mr Shuffleton's Allegorical Survey of the Scottish Poets of the Present Day'. Of all the parts in *The Spy*, as he admits in the concluding issue, these were the ones that gave 'the greatest personal offence'. A friend of the Spy introduces Mr Shuffleton, a strange man who 'supposes every poet's muse his mistress, or *sweetheart*; . . . and in this large mirror here, or rather in that magic area seemingly behind it, he makes these ladies to appear'. This fictional framework will enable Hogg to assess the relation of style to meaning, and the attitude towards nature and physical reality, in the poets he discusses. Shuffleton then introduces the muses of the two most popular Scottish poets of the day, Scott and Thomas Campbell. Dancing to 'a wild irregular measure', Scott's mistress enters 'in such a hop-step-and-jump pace', says Mr Spy, 'that I could hardly believe the lady to be in her right senses'. He explains that her 'majesty and beauty' seem incompatible with her 'wildness'. Campbell's sweetheart is equally disappointing, a statuesque woman who at

25

first glance appears 'noble and graceful' but soon begins 'to look paler, and somewhat enfeebled'.

Luckily there is also a third young woman, infinitely superior, whom we soon recognise as the muse of James Hogg. 'A country-looking girl', with 'an old faithful colley', she first appears wearing a mantle like that of Scott's mistress, 'but finding that it rather incumbered her, she threw it off, and appeared in the dress of a native shepherdess'. In contrast to the previous two muses, it is found that this third woman becomes more and more beautiful 'in proportion to the minuteness of our inspection'. 'What a pity it is', says Mr Spy, 'that this girl is not more attentive to her dress'. — 'A self-willed imp', retorts Shuffleton, 'who thinks more of her accomplishments than any other body does; and because her taste is natural, thinks it infallible'. Although she has a chequered past, this likeable, attractive woman at least understands the importance of nature and spontaneity. Her future looks very bright, with Mr Shuffleton willing to 'lay any bet, that this Shepherdess will pay more attention to the regularity and elegance of her dress . . . and learn by experience that cooks must not always make dishes to their own taste'.

Many of the stories in *The Spy* reflect obliquely and ironically on the personality of its editor. One correspondent (actually Hogg himself) solemnly lectures Mr Spy on 'The Danger of Changing Occupations', and then recounts his own failings as an erstwhile apprentice, shepherd, violinist, shopkeeper, and farmer. Again the theme is man's relation to the physical and economic world, as the correspondent recalls his humiliating descent from power to dependence and fear. His farming venture failed because he 'played upon the fiddle' too often; 'the servants joined in the same laxity and mirth; left the door half open, and danced to my music in the kitchen. I saw my folly as usual, but could not remedy it'. He even persuaded his housekeeper, 'as the night was so long, and so cold, . . . to take a share of my bed until it was day'. 'I found I was no more master of my own house', he complains; 'I had voluntarily brought myself down to a level' with the servants. With his farm failing and his housekeeper pregnant, the hero decided to escape from the economic, social and physical circumstances which his actions had brought about. He then sailed to Québec, where he fought against the Americans in 1775. In the new world the hero was haunted by the same difficulties in a new form, with nightmarish images of bullets, physical pain, and even landscape combining to diminish further his precarious self-image:

I was fully convinced, before I had ever seen a battle, I should be a most notorious coward myself. I could not even bear the idea of bullets whizzing by my ears, or striking up the turf and dust hard by where I stood; and thought my love of life and fear of pain would induce me to take the first opportunity of getting out of their way. And moreover, whenever I dreamed of a battle in my sleep, which I frequently did, my invariable custom was to squat behind some adjacent dike or hillock, and await in perfect safety the issue of the dreadful affray.

This tale has affinities with 'The Mistakes of a Night', 'Dialogue in a Country Church-Yard', and many of Mr Spy's mishaps, all of which undermine the concept of individuality by conducting a protagonist down into a physical world which is at first inviting but soon shows itself to be an irrational, frightening realm of confusion, the nightmare, and chaos. James Hogg has yet to find a way of convincingly resolving the issues, and 'The Danger of Changing Occupations' ends simply with the hero's return to Scotland and his admission of former errors.

Seventy-three readers (nearly one in four) indignantly cancelled their subscriptions to *The Spy* after reading of this correspondent's adventures with his housekeeper. Another anonymous letter, actually written by Scott on Hogg's behalf, hastened to assure subscribers that *The Spy* was only trying 'to paint the truth' so as to expose 'a detestable course of life', adding that in future Mr Spy would be wise to avoid stories 'which may . . . injure the cause of morality, or add the slightest tint of the rose-leaf to the modest cheek'.[2] Still, parts of the offending tale, as Dr Browne informs us, were widely reported to be 'a *sketch* of [Hogg's] own *life* up to the time of his coming to Edinburgh — *and a more shameful and indecent paper was never laid so barefacedly before the public*'.[3] Meanwhile Mr Spy promises to obey Scott's '*severe, but perhaps too just*' reprimand, yet shortly before Christmas he offers readers a lusty account of his youthful love adventures under the title 'Misery of an Old Batchelor'.

In this story Mr Spy recalls that his first love affair began while reading *The Vicar of Wakefield* with a young woman of high social standing:

> She commonly run over the pages faster than I could, but always refrained from turning the leaf until I cried — *Now*. I still could not see very well, and crept a little closer to her side. I even found it necessary, in order to *see* with *precision*, to bring my cheek almost close to her's. . . . We came to the end of a chapter — *Now*, said I; but it seems I had said it in a different way that time, for instead of turning the leaf, she closed the book! This little adverb has many various meanings, all of which are easily distinguished by the manner of pronouncing it. I am weary of it, said she. — 'Tis time, said I. I envied not the joy of angels that day!

When young Mr Spy declared his passion, the woman replied,

> 'The sea, to be sure, is very deep, but he is a great coward who dares not wade to the knee in it!' — What do you say, Madam? said I — she repeated the sentence. But do you say that in earnest? said I. Indeed I do, said she, firmly; while her eyes were fixed on the ground. I clasped her to my bosom. . . .

Much of the humour here consists in the juxtaposition of a polite or educated social facade with the deeper, fluid, oceanic reality of physical passion.

Another sweetheart indicated to the young Spy that 'the night season was the best' for amorous meetings. 'Perhaps my Edinburgh readers will be startled', he comments, 'but it is a fact, that every young woman in the country must be courted by night, or else they will not be courted at all'. From this second mistress the Spy received a treatment that foreshadows his fall into a pool while chasing women in Edinburgh: pretending to help him escape from her jealous father, she opened her second-story window, and, taking 'hold of my father's chequered plaid, . . . desired me to let myself down by it', promising solemnly 'that she would hold by one end until I reached the ground'. For some unexplained reason, 'the very moment on which I slid from the window stone, and began to lay my weight to the plaid, down came the window with a crack like a pistol!' The window, the fall, and the mocking young woman's ambivalent and enigmatic character, are all precursors of what happens to the Spy many years later in Edinburgh, when he falls into the pool of water.

The tone of *The Spy* was always unpredictable. At times James Hogg seems determined to appease his respectable readers, yet at other times he throws off restraint and writes with surprising freedom. One week would bring safe, sentimental ballads, or a lecture from Mr Spy on 'the urgent necessity of a speedy reformation in life and manners', while another might bring tales of passion or indelicate allusions such as the following description of the mistresses of certain poets:

> 'But pray, Mr Shuffleton', said [the Spy's] friend . . . 'what is the meaning of the huge bunches of trumpery which these ladies wear upon their rumps? That is surely a new fashion. . . .'
>
> 'These', said [Shuffleton], 'are worn merely for the sake of adding to their bulk. . . . Without these, Sir, they could never be put to bed, for they would not fill *one pair of sheets*; nor if put to bed could they ever rise again, as it would be a shame to appear without *stays* in public, and their slender bodies would be quite lost in them. These things, Sir, the ladies call *notes*, and they are the very tip-top of the fashion. . . .'

The comparison here is between two kinds of padding: the *notes* with which stylish young women fill out their underwear, and the *footnotes* with which stylish poets fill out their volumes of poetry.

Mr Spy's 'Story of Two Highlanders' is a thinly-disguised allegory of his difficult relations with subscribers. The two Highlanders have emigrated to 'the banks of the Albany River, which falls into Hudson's Bay', where, 'to their infinite joy, they discovered a deep pit, or cavern, which contained a large litter of fine half-grown pigs'. Donald stands outside as the smaller man enters the den and begins to club the piglets. Suddenly 'a monstrous wild boar' appears, 'roaring, and grinding his tusks, while the fire of rage gleamed from his eyes'. The boar tries to enter his den, at which the man outside 'laid hold of his large,

29

long tail — wrapped it around both his hands, . . . and held back in the utmost desperation'.

Words like 'boar' and 'pig' were common nicknames for James Hogg. The piglets of this story seem to represent Hogg's literary productions, which the smaller man, like an outrageously moralistic critic, butchers. Hogg is angered by the way his offspring are received, but his need to appease his remaining subscribers (represented by the larger man) prevents him from coming to the defence of the poor piglets. Afterwards the lucky Highlanders derive great pleasure from their heartless massacre: 'During the long winter nights, while the family were regaling themselves on the hams of the great wild boar, often was the above tale related, and as often applauded, and laughed at'. Like his *Confessions*, thirteen years later, Hogg's 'Story of Two Highlanders' expresses and transforms into art the exasperation he felt with his Edinburgh readers and critics.

Most of Hogg's prose fictions begin with a protagonist who makes great claims to individuality, whether through social position, talent, passion, beauty, or religion. This hero or heroine is then made to endure social, economic, or physical realities, and then is conducted on a further descent, which may be either funny or horrifying, into extreme chaos and mystery. A good example is 'Love of Fame', in *The Spy*, where Hogg introduces a handsome, aristocratic, and intelligent youth named Adam Bell. Adam 'often boasted aloud' and 'valued himself particularly upon his skill in the broadsword exercise'. Mysteriously he sets out from his estate in 1745, probably to join the Jacobite Rebellion. The hero then simply disappears, leaving the narrator unable to decide between different explanations. When someone resembling Adam appears briefly, the narrator tells us that this may be a ghost, or a thief dressed in Adam's clothes, or the hero himself in disguise. 'But the causes which produced the events here related', he concludes, 'have never been accounted for in this world; even conjecture is left to wander in a labyrinth'.

Years later a report of a fatal duel in Edinburgh becomes the likeliest explanation for Adam Bell's disappearance. The event had been witnessed by a solitary man hiding 'in the shadow of the wall' on a night when 'The moon shone so bright that it was almost as light as noon-day'. He recalls that a young, athletic swordsman appeared to have the advantage over his older, fat opponent, until 'his foot slipped, and he stumbled forward towards his antagonist, who . . . met his breast . . . with the point of his sword, and run him through the body'.

Similar duel scenes often occur in Hogg's major works, as for instance 'Basil Lee', *The Three Perils of Woman*, and the *Confessions of a Justified Sinner*. The duels usually take place on moonlit nights in a small, open area, a clearly-defined foreground surrounded by darkness. There is generally a witness, hidden and silent, and in most cases the duel is fatal. One of the duellists must of course be the proud, pretentious protagonist. The duel inevitably occurs at a low point on the hero's and reader's journey through the irrational, the inhuman world of extreme chaos or mystery. For James Hogg the swordfight brings a sudden moment of clarity in contrast to the indeterminate, shadowy world that surrounds it. It symbolises the author's conviction that all people are essentially equal, or in other words that the hero's pretensions to superiority are false. The details about Hogg's duels are often unclear, but the main fact is that one self must confront another self in a struggle for life.

Another tale in *The Spy*, 'Evil Speaking Ridiculed by an Allegorical Dream', is the first of Hogg's works to suggest a convincing way of escaping from chaos. This comic piece takes the form of a short letter to Mr Spy, informing him of the correspondent's visit to the caustic and pessimistic Mr A. T., a local philosopher. An old, frustrated bachelor, Mr A. T. has much in common with Mr Spy, except that his outlook is objective and rationalistic, the very opposite of the editor's vaunted subjectivity. A. T. freely condemns the people of Edinburgh as 'depraved reprobates, and the slaves of sin and Satan'. The women of Edinburgh, he has found, are 'all slaves to the worst of passions'. The naively sentimental correspondent, by contrast, speaks of 'our ladies' as 'those sweet, those amiable creatures, whom I had always fondly viewed as that link in the chain of creation which connected the angelic with the human nature'.

As he listens to Mr A. T.'s wide-ranging denunciations, the correspondent falls asleep and dreams that his host turns into a clergyman, a pig, and, at the same time, Satan:

> At length a tall lady stretched forward her head, and whispered to me that he was the devil. I uttered a loud scream,

31

and hid myself behind the pew, having a peculiar aversion to that august personage, and peeping through a hole, I beheld him change his form gradually from that of a human creature, into a huge black sow. He then stepped down from the pulpit, with some difficulty, and began feeding out of a deep trough. A thought struck me in a moment, that I might easily rid mankind of their greatest enemy, by felling him at one blow before he observed me . . . ; so, snatching down a grave-pole, I glided silently away to execute my cowardly purpose. . . . At that very moment he lifted up his ugly phiz! and gave me such a look, that I was quite overcome with terror, and fled yelling along the area, and the devil after me. My knees grew extremely weak, and besides I was so entangled among women and petticoats, that I sunk powerless to the earth, and Satan got hold of me by the arm. My friend, at that unlucky moment, observing my extraordinary agitation, took hold of my arm, and awaked me. My scattered senses not having got time to collect, I still conceived him to be the devil, and . . . I attacked my astonished friend with the most determined fury, boxing him unmercifully on the face, and uttering the most dreadful imprecations, resolved, it seems, that he should not insult me, or take me prisoner with impunity.

Both Mr A. T. and the correspondent endure a dramatic descent from the human to the subhuman worlds, according to the logic of this dream. The proud, arrogant philosopher forfeits his personal identity and stability, to become a split personality whose nature shifts uncertainly between male and female, and between human, animal, and demonic. The dreamer also forfeits his normal identity, screaming and upsetting the congregation, running with terror, being trapped by women, attacking his friend, and suffering 'scattered senses'.

Afterwards the contrite letter-writer imagines that the 'accident was a kind of judgment inflicted on us both for a dangerous error; on him for abusing so many of the human race behind their backs, who were in all probability better than he; and on me for assenting implicitly to all his injurious insinuations'. People who try in effect to separate themselves from the rest of humanity, either through the pride of objective reason or the pride of indulgent sentimentality or subjectivity, then, are in danger of losing human identity and a stable personality. For the first time, James Hogg is able to show the equal limitations of both the objective and subjective points-of-view. He transcends those partial perspectives in the simple, profound realisation of the unity of 'the human race'. The correspondent now sees the arrogant Mr A. T. as a 'limb . . . of the devil' and converts to a more generous outlook which affirms 'a higher opinion of the dignity of human nature'. In 'Evil Speaking' Hogg presents in full for the first time his characteristic personal myth of descent: the journey downwards into extreme confusion dissolves pretensions, separate identities, and false values, but finally leads to a firm (that is, universal) basis for authentic order, identity, and value, through the simple admission that all people are essentially the same.

The Spy was a tremendous artistic success for James Hogg. It brought him beyond the contrasting limitations of rationalism and emotion, and gave him his keynote theme of human unity, fellowship, and social vision. Unfortunately, as Mr Spy concedes in the final number,

> The learned, the enlightened, and polite circles of this flourishing metropolis, disdained either to be amused or instructed by the ebulitions of humble genius. Enemies, swelling with the most rancorous spite, grunted in every corner; and from none has the Spy suffered so much injury and blame, as from some pretended friends, who were indeed liberal in their advices, and ardent in their professions of friendship, yet took every method in their power to lessen the work in the esteem of others, by branding its author with designs the most subversive of all civility and decorum.

'At that period the whole of the aristocracy and literature of Scotland both high and low', Hogg later explained, 'were set against me and determined to keep me down'.[4]

Two very helpful friends at this time, however, were James Gray and his wife Mary. They were an older couple, very proud of having known Robert Burns many years before, and they both contributed several pieces to *The Spy*. Gray was a classics teacher in Edinburgh. His influence on Hogg accounts for the many classical quotations, in Latin or English, in *The Spy*. 'Truly zealous for the honour and fame of the Shepherd, Gray wished him to read and study', writes Robert Gillies; Hogg, in response, 'took up by rote divers of Gray's Latin phrases, and in his prose writings used to table them at haphazard'.[5]

Well over half of *The Spy*'s fifty-two issues begin with a classical quotation. The authors include Plautus (twice), Cicero, Homer, Martial, Virgil (three times), Seneca, Juvenal (twice), and Ovid (twice). But the main influence is from Horace, who appears at the head of eleven essays, and is sometimes quoted within individual stories. The Roman satirist evidently exerted a strong sway over Hogg's development as an artist; Horace's influence can be seen in the graceful negligence, the quiet ironies, and the provocative comparisons, of the mature works of James Hogg.

Hogg was forty when *The Spy* died in September 1811. He continued to read and study, and helped to found an educational society called The Forum. 'I never was so much advantaged', he later wrote, 'by any thing as by that society; for it let me feel . . . the pulse of the public, and precisely what they would swallow, and what they would not'. For three years, between five hundred and fifteen hundred men and women paid sixpence each week to hear the Shepherd and his friends discuss philosophical and social issues. Everyone voted after the debate, and the money raised went to charities like the Female Society, Destitute Sick Society, Deaf and Dumb Institution, and a number of schools. Hogg's friends 'were averse to my coming forward in the Forum as a public speaker, and tried to reason me out of it, by representing my incapacity to harangue a thousand people in a speech of half an hour'. However, the Shepherd's 'confidence in myself being unbounded, I began, and came off with flying colours'.

Undoubtedly The Forum was a great help in Hogg's development as a thinker. As well as being a founding member and also an elected official, James Hogg says that he 'spoke every night', and afterwards helped to distribute the charity.[6] Most Edinburgh newspapers carried reports of The Forum's activities:

> Several gentlemen belonging to The Forum, have . . .
> called at the jail of this city, and, after making inquiry into
> the conduct of the prisoners, paid Captain SIBBALD the sum

of eight guineas, to be applied by him to the relief of the most necessitous; by which means several persons, incarcerated for small sums, have been released.

FORUM.—The question last night—'*Whether the hope of Reward or the fear of Punishment tends most to the preservation of good order in Society?*'—was decided in favour of reward. The Treasurer has paid . . . Twenty Pounds to the funds of the Lunatic Asylum. The proceeds of a previous night have been distributed among upwards of twenty poor families.[7]

One witness at these weekly debates recalls an evening when Hogg spoke on the folly of matrimony. Hogg suddenly forgot what he was saying, 'and, after some instants of breathless suspence', pulled a sheaf of notes from his pocket and held them near the candle. When someone complained of the delay, 'Hogg coolly snuffed the candle, which was attached to the adjoining pillar, and . . . said, with the utmost composure, 'What's a' the hurry?''[8] Although Hogg thought he was 'in general a prodigious favourite',[9] a very different interpretation comes from the ex-preacher, ex-lawyer, and ex-editor Dr James Browne, who writes that his 'grotesque . . . exhibitions' made him the 'clown or merryandrew' of The Forum.

Economically these were years of failure for James Hogg. He was now reduced to accepting food, clothes, and shelter from a few kind supporters. According to one story passed along by the unrelenting Dr Browne, Hogg at one time applied to The Forum

for a sum of £10, which he alleged was for the use of some poor family that had come under his notice . . . but such was the *distrust of his coadjutors*, that this was refused, *unless another party accompanied Mr. Hogg in giving away the money*. Mr. Hogg *prudently* declined this, and *so the matter ended*.[10]

Notes

1 Hogg, 'Epitaphs on Living Characters', *Scots Magazine*, June 1810, p. 447.
2 'Letter to the Spy on his Former Numbers', *Spy*, 13 Oct. 1810, pp. 55-56.

3   '*Life*' of the Ettrick Shepherd Anatomized, p. 17.
4   Hogg, *Anecdotes of Sir W. Scott*, p. 47.
5   Gillies, *Memoirs of a Literary Veteran*, 3 vols. (London, 1851), III, 54.
6   Hogg, 'Memoir', p. 23.
7   Anon. notices in *Edinburgh Weekly Chronicle*, 4 Mar. 1812, n.p., and *Edinburgh Star*, 17 Apr. 1812, n.p.
8   Anon., "What's a' the Hurry?'; A Reminiscence of the Ettrick Shepherd', *Edinburgh Literary Journal*, 2 Oct. 1830, p. 220.
9   Hogg, 'Memoir', p. 23.
10 '*Life*' of the Ettrick Shepherd Anatomized, pp. 40, 39.

Chapter Three

THE FRAME IS BRACED, THE MIND SET FREE

IN a rented room in the suburbs of Edinburgh, in a 'weather-beaten, rather ghostly, solitary' building 'like an old farmhouse',[1] where the landlord got drunk every evening and beat his wife, James Hogg wrote his first long poem. Almost a year before its publication, Edinburgh readers were being advised that 'Mr. Hogg, the 'Etterick Shepherd,' is preparing for publication a Legendary Tale called the 'Queen's Wake,' in ten cantos'.[2] Six months later the city learned that the Shepherd had 'made considerable progress',[3] and finally on February 5th, 1813, a front-page notice in the *Edinburgh Advertiser* proclaimed 'This day is published, Elegantly printed in octavo, price 12s. boards, and on royal paper, price 21s. boards, THE QUEEN'S WAKE, a LEGENDARY POEM'. A banquet 'in honour of the occasion'[4] was given by Hogg's friend John Grieve, on the day of publication.

The ballad, with its obvious simplicity and economy, and its use of stock situations and reliance on external action, has seldom been highly regarded as an art form. In *The Queen's Wake* Hogg turns these weaknesses to his own advantage, achieving lucidity by combining his twelve separate ballads in a structure that challenges readers to notice broad parallels, echoes, and ironies. It was apparently this combination of simplicity and suggestiveness which prompted the dramatist Maturin to rate Hogg as his second-favourite poet of the age:

His Queen's Wake is a splendid and impassioned work. I like it for its varieties, and its utter simplicity.[5]

James Hogg was well aware of the limitations of traditional ballad form. He often makes fun of his primitive balladeers, as for example when one breathless bard delivers his tale of 'Macgregor':

Loud, and more loud, the minstrel sung;
Loud, and more loud, the chords he rung;
Wild grew his looks, for well he knew
The scene was dread, the tale was true!
And ere Loch Ketturine's wave was won,
Faultered his voice, his breath was done.

Similar clanging rhythms, dense Gothic hyperbole, and comic
bathos are ironically presented in 'King Edward's Dream', whose
schoolteacher minstrel assumes that everyone will share his
enthusiasm:

'Twas all unequalled, and would make
Immortal bards! immortal wake!
About Dunedin streets he ran,
Each knight he met, each maid, each man,
In field, in alley, tower, or hall,
The wake was first, the wake was all.

Not only does this bard's excitement overthrow his grammar, but
he sings 'so bold and high, / While patriot fire flashed from his
eye', that he too loses his voice and is led from the stage in painful
silence.

The main theme of *The Queen's Wake* is the nature of adversity.
Hogg looks at adversity from an objective perspective, through
the historical sufferings of the Scottish people, and from a
subjective perspective, through his own sufferings as a man and
an artist. These two aspects of adversity are symbolised in the
metaphor of the storm, which (with one important exception)
recurs in different ways in each of the ballads. There is bleak
irony in the fact that the poet's opening lines address — not a
patron, audience, or muse, but — simply 'Winter clouds', which
he sees as adversaries:

Now burst, ye Winter clouds that lower,
Fling from your folds the piercing shower;
Sing to the tower and leafless tree,
Ye cold winds of adversity;
Your blights, your chilling influence shed,
On wareless heart, and houseless head;
Your ruth or fury I disdain,
I've found my Mountain Lyre again.

In his defiance of the storm and his recognition of its destructive power, the poet stands opposed to nature. The self is dwarfed by its natural surroundings, yet through creativity it remains autonomous, free, and capable, a source of power in its own right. Imagination, symbolised by the poet's harp or lyre, is therefore a 'gift of heaven', a 'pledge of good', enabling him to withstand 'cold winds'. Throughout *The Queen's Wake* the storm represents hardship, warfare, change, chaos, and history. Queen Mary's reign, like the other historical periods depicted in the different ballads, is only 'a passing shower'.

The other sustained image is the notion of form, which expresses Hogg's hope that through art human experience can be given a more meaningful shape. The arts purify the soul; they bring verticality, order, harmony of parts, beauty, contentment, and finally freedom. A herald tells us in the Introduction that

> None draws the soul so sweet away,
> As music's melting mystic lay;
> Slight emblem of the bliss above,
> It soothes the spirit all to love.
>
> To cherish this attractive art,
> To lull the passions, mend the heart,
> And break the moping zealot's chains,
> Hear what our lovely Queen ordains.

Form is the opposite of the storm, the chaos, yet it can only be attained by enduring the storm. Thus the Italian bard Rizzio, weak and effeminate, is clearly lacking in the qualities of soul necessary to an artist, since his 'glossy eye and lady form / Had never braved the northern storm'. On the other hand the eleven Scottish bards are more acquainted with adversity, and 'Not stern December's fierce controul / Could quench the flame of minstrel's soul'. Frequent images of circles (— the first bard sings to a 'courtly circle', while the fourth speaks of a 'magic ring' and 'circling years' —) remind us of the poet's search for form, and contribute to the loose unity of *The Queen's Wake*.

Against this symbolic background James Hogg imagines his series of ballads, each sung at the court of Mary Queen of Scots in Edinburgh, on three successive nights in 1561. As the ending will prove, Hogg wants his readers to see the whole, to perceive connections between the separate ballads, between the various journeys and battles depicted, and between the three main sections of the poem.

The three ballads of 'Night the First' give three perspectives on the journey motif: a failure to undertake a necessary journey, in the first, a guilty flight, in the second, and a demonic voyage towards death, in the third. The first is the tale of Malcolm of Lorn, who stays with his mother instead of going with his lover as she leaves for her new home on the continent. 'He clung to his parent, and sunk on the strand', and afterwards dies in despair. Malcolm refuses the voyage, and is destroyed by the past, in the shape of his mother and his memories. This is the song recited by the Italian weakling Rizzio, and it expresses Rizzio's hope that Scotland will remain loyal to Rome and tie itself to the continent rather than asserting its independent nationhood. But from the point-of-view of James Hogg, this is the one ballad which takes no account of the storm and the independent qualities required to weather the storm.

The hero of the second ballad, 'Young Kennedy', has experienced too much of the storm, instead of too little. Even in childhood he was 'hushed by the tempest, baptized with the rain', and 'loud winter-torrents his lullaby sung'. Kennedy simply internalises the storm's destructive capacity, killing an old man so that he can marry the man's daughter. The father's ghost then appears at their wedding bed, and Kennedy flees in horror, before finally committing suicide. Kennedy and his bride have tried to deny the past, whereas Malcolm, in the earlier ballad, had tied himself to the past; both extremes end in defeat for a pair of lovers.

This suggests that to be dominated by former times, or to try to ignore the past altogether, are equally wrong. Only the poet and the bards, in these tales, enjoy a strengthening, genuine relationship with past times, through their shared experience of creativity and their ability to envision scenes from the past. The poet, Hogg, tells us that he has sung these verses 'On Ettrick banks', where he felt that

> The spirit of the bard was nigh;
> Swung by the breeze on braken pile,
> Or hovering o'er me with a smile.

40

Imagination, then, is a way of keeping the past alive, learning from the past, and using a sense of the past to alleviate or redeem the present moment.

The third ballad is Hogg's famous, funny, 'Witch of Fife'. In this piece the past is represented by its archaic, fifteenth-century language. An old man, married to a witch, overhears her secret incantation, repeats the words himself, and follows her on her midnight journey to the Bishop of Carlisle's castle.

> They flew to the vaultis of merry Carlisle,   vaults
>   Quhair they enterit free as ayr;   Where
> And they drank and they drank of the byshopis wyne
>   Quhill they culde drynk ne mair.   'Till

His wife leaves the old man asleep on the Bishop's floor, where soldiers find him the next morning:

> 'Now quha are ye, ye silly auld man,   who
>   That sleepis se sound and se weil?
> Or how gat ye into the bishopis vault
>   Throu lokkis and barris of steel?'—
>
> The auld gude-man he tryit to speak,
>   But ane word he culdna fynde;
> He tryit to think, but his head whirlit round,
>   And ane thing he culdna mynde:—
> 'I cam fra Fyfe,' the auld man cryit,
> 'And I cam on the midnycht wynde.'

The old man is then tied to a stake and burned to death. Like the previous two heroes, he becomes ultimately a victim of his own desires. He, too, is trapped within a particular moment of time, whereas the bard, thanks to imagination and historical perspective, supposedly enjoys a freedom from the bondage of past or present.

'Night the First' is a kind of *Inferno*. Its main characters are imprisoned by history, memory, or narrow desires. With 'Night the Second' we enter a kind of *Purgatorio* where mankind struggles, in general with increasing success, to work free of its chains, to redeem the present, and somehow to have contact with the infinite.

41

D

The first ballad on this second evening is 'The Spirit of the Storm', a legend of a Highland seer who has communed with spirits and is about to see 'what mortal could not bear'. As he stands conjuring, 'Firm in his magic ring', the seer unintentionally raises 'The giant Spirit of the Storm':

> Red, red and grizzly were his eyes;
>   His cap the moon-cloud's silver gray;
> His staff the writhed snake, that lies
>   Pale, bending o'er the milky way.

The seer tries to withstand this destructive presence, but the spirit rips the seer's 'arctic ring . . . asunder' and kills him. The Spirit of the Storm symbolises the centuries of warfare and horror that will plague Scotland in the wake of Queen Mary. Because he holds tightly and rigidly to an inadequate notion of form (cowering within a 'ring' which in this case tries to exclude the storm, the chaos) the 'feeble' seer of course dies.

The fifth minstrel, a shepherd from Ettrick, stands for James Hogg himself.

> The ladies smiled, the courtiers sneered;
> For such a simple air and mien
> Before a court had never been.
> A clown he was, bred in the wild,
> And late from native moors exiled.

Perhaps because this simple bard has felt 'Nature's grand turmoil', and 'His eye had seen the thunder-storm', he is the first to recount a successful journey. He tells of an old man who spies a troop of fairies on a hillside. At first the old man delights in watching them, with thoughts of 'riding on the wind', 'Of sailing lightly o'er the sea',

> Or through the sounding spheres to sing,
> Borne on the fiery meteor's wing;
> . . .
> And then he thought — O! dread to tell!—
> Of tithes the fairies paid to hell!

42

With his 'reverend eye' towards heaven, Old David calls on his seven sons to search the fairies' den in secret. The person David had thought was the Fairy Queen turns out to be a human, the beautiful Ann of Raeburn, held prisoner 'here in this dark and drear abode'. The fairies are then defeated when they return to their underground den. Ann is freed from her prison, and at the end she marries one of David's sons. The riches which the fairies had stolen are returned to their human owners. This song cunningly echoes many features of 'The Witch of Fife', except that its hero succeeds in subduing the demonic forces. There still remains, however, a deep division between the human and spiritual, which will only be resolved in the third section of *The Queen's Wake*.

The next ballad combines the two motifs of journey and battle. A warrior named Macgregor, lured away by the spirit of a woman he had wronged many years before, deserts his friends on the eve of a battle. The woman's spirit then places Macgregor on a boat that takes him 'in horror and pain' to a 'dark lake' where he disappears 'for ever and ay'.

Macgregor deserts his fellow-warriors and is destroyed by his own past, by a demonic presence, and by his guilty imagination. '[T]hy fancies are wild as the wind', a friend warns him; 'The dreams of the night have disordered thy mind'. His imagination is borne away, engulfed, and annihilated, by the wind that carries him to the dark lake.

Yet whatever happens to Macgregor, the tone of the ballad remains optimistic, since its bard is inspired by a vision of both 'that was past, and that should be'. The difference between Macfarlane (the minstrel) and Macgregor (the victim) is neatly implied in the contrast between the weather-wise shepherd, able to predict storms, and, secondly, the younger, inexperienced shepherd, for whom storms always come as a surprise. The first, the wise shepherd, knows when a storm is coming and when 'the gathering cloud / Shall all his noontide glories shroud'. The second man, not having learned from the past and therefore unable to foresee the future,

> Sees not coming rains and wind,
> The beacon of the dawning hour,
> Nor notes the blink before the shower.

43

At this point Hogg plays a joke on his readers and critics, ending the ballad so abruptly that his audience is caught, like incompetent farmers, unprepared for the storm. The bad sheep-farmer, we are told,

> Astonished, mid his open grain,
> Sees round him pour the sudden rain,—
> So looked the still attentive throng,
> When closed at once Macfarlane's song.

In these last two lines Queen Mary's courtiers are brilliantly transformed into the unimaginative critics of 1813. Both the sixteenth-century courtiers and the nineteenth-century critics are apparently incapable of foreseeing the storm, or of understanding the thematic pattern, the form, of *The Queen's Wake*.

'Macgregor' tells of a battle missed, but the next song, 'Earl Walter', tells of a youth who bravely goes to fight an opponent 'Whom man could never tame'. The opponent is Lord Darcie, a Frenchman, older, stronger, and more experienced, with whom Walter must joust before a royal court. It appears certain that the younger man will die, but to everyone's surprise he beats Darcie, then shows mercy and allows him to live. Symbolically this resolution corresponds to one of the basic historical 'lessons' of the whole poem: in effect the hero frees himself from domination by the past, while also avoiding the opposite extreme of trying to annihilate or deny the past.

'Kilmeny', the last ballad of 'Night the Second', turns again to the fifteenth-century language of Henryson and Dunbar. Kilmeny is a 'Sinless virgin, free of stain', who, taken by angels to heaven, learns 'Of the tymes that are now, and the tymes that shall be'. She sees the sufferings that will be brought about by John Knox (a 'gruff grim keryl') and by the French Revolution, and then

> scho saw quhill the sorrouis of man war bye,   she saw 'till
> And all was lufe and hermonye;   love
> Quhill the sternis of hevin fell lownly away,   Till the stars
> Lyke the flekis of snaw on a winter day.

Here at the exact centre of *The Queen's Wake* is the vision of harmony and stillness, an ideal centre-of-gravity in the turning world of journeys and battles. 'Unless there is such a center', as Northrop Frye suggests (in a different context) 'there is nothing to prevent the analogies supplied by convention and genre from being an endless series of free associations', an 'endless labyrinth without an outlet'.[6] Kilmeny provides the focal point which Queen Mary, as a careful reading will discover, abundantly and quite disastrously fails to supply.

Relaxed rhythms, peaceful images, and a suggestive use of triplets, separate 'Kilmeny' from the other songs:

> Als still was her luke, and als still was her ee,   As
> Als the stilnesse that lay on the emerant lee,
> Or the myst that sleips on ane waveless sea.

From this 'everlestyng dreime' Kilmeny one day returns to Scotland to warn of the difficult future: the animals welcome her, forming a 'pecefu ryng' as she sings, but the people only react with 'fiere and dreide'. Like 'The Spirit of the Storm', 'Old David', and 'Macgregor', the ballad of 'Kilmeny' stresses the divorce between human and spiritual:

> Scho left this worild of sorrow and paine,
> And returnit to the land of thochte againe.

As the second night ends, Queen Mary warns her courtiers to beware 'that hideous form, / The ruthless angel of the storm'. The next morning,

> The storm had ceased to shroud the hill;
> The morning's breath was pure and chill.

Metaphors and personifications are more benign for most of 'Night the Third', to suggest that natural and spiritual forces have now been brought into harmony with (corrected) human desires. The storm now gives way to the inspiring breeze, as a symbol for the poet's creative energy. Apparently the endurance of bad weather gives the human personality a certain form, which is the precondition to freedom of mind. On this third morning, then,

> The frame was braced, the mind set free
> To feat, or brisk hilarity.

45

The mind is a prisoner of the body, and therefore of the natural and physical world, until it is 'set free' by attaining a properly 'braced' frame, or form. Paradoxically, a sense of form brings liberation from form, or from arbitrary boundaries; this is implied in Hogg's use of images of motion (such as 'set free' and 'brisk' in the couplet above) to describe the movement of consciousness.

'Night the Third' begins with outdoor celebrations by the courtiers. The two sports in which they engage deftly symbolise the two major motifs of the whole poem. The first is curling, in which

> The Highland chief, the Border knight,
> In waving plumes, and baldricks bright,
> Join in the bloodless friendly war,
> The sounding-stone to hurl afar.

If the first sport presents a redeemed image of the battle, the second supplies, naturally, a redeemed image of the journey or flight:

> The youth, on cramps of polished steel,   blades
> Joined in the race, the curve, the wheel;
> With arms outstretched, and foot aside,
> Like lightning o'er the lake they glide;
> And eastward far their impulse keep,
> Like angels journeying o'er the deep.

Human, natural, and divine are brought together in these celebrations, as are also Highland and Lowland, youth and age, and male and female.

Harmony is restored in 'Night the Third', although the repercussions of this are not always welcomed by individuals. In the first ballad, Lord Pringle is in love with Mary Scott, the daughter of a rival chieftain. Pringle disguises himself as an Abbot to be near her, and is then arrested by her father, imprisoned, and sentenced for execution. Mary, however, dresses up as an angel to release him:

> Fair was the form that o'er him hung,
> And fair the hands that set him free;
> The trembling whispers of her tongue
> Softer than seraph's melody.

Mary's parents then give her poison, to punish her for loving their enemy, and a battle ensues between the armies of the two chiefs. Although Pringle is victorious, he finds Mary already apparently dead, but when he kisses her the effect of the drug wears off and she returns to life. A marriage follows, together with pledges of friendship between the two groups.

In this piece the heroine, and Scottish society in general, are freed from a bitter past. A similar resolution occurs in the next ballad, 'King Edward's Dream', where the English monarch, conquering and pillaging in Scotland, has a dream which correctly predicts his own death and the resurrection of a free, united Scotland.

In the second-last ballad the Scots have been defeated by the English, and young Morison of Locherben has died while protecting his sister. Douglas, the Scottish leader, then woos Morison's sister as she kneels weeping over her brother's corpse. 'His soul thou never canst recal', Douglas tells her, but she replies,

> Go, first thy flocks and herds regain;
> Revenge thy friends in battle slain;
> Thy wounded honour heal; that done,
> Douglas may ask May Morison.

The two lovers have opposite responses to past events: Douglas wants to ignore the significance of the past and the need to correct injustices that survive from the past, while May, at the opposite extreme, is obsessed with the past, as she mourns her brother and demands revenge. The impasse is resolved when Douglas, roused by May's rebuke, defeats the invaders and regains the stolen goods, asserts the freedom of Scotland, and finally marries May. In the context of *The Queen's Wake* as a whole this implies that the present can free itself from the past only through a proper understanding of the past, an understanding which neither tries to deny the lessons of history, nor is obsessed with the bitter legacies of history.

The last ballad, 'The Abbot McKinnon', is the best. A sinful, lecherous Abbot of Iona has a dream in which his patron saint

> Bade him arise from his guilty sleep,
> And pay his respects to the God of the deep.

The ironies of this command are not evident to the Abbot. With his crew of like-minded monks he sails to the island of Staffa, where a kind of natural 'temple' has been sculpted by 'the waves of the angry sea'. The scene has some affinities with the visit to Stonehenge near the end of *Tess of the D'Urbervilles*:

> The solemn rows in that darksome den,
> Were dimly seen like the forms of men,
> Like giant monks in ages agone,
> Whom the God of the ocean had seared to stone.

Here the prehistoric past, the human past, the present, nature, and the divine are united in the image of rocks shaped by the God of the ocean into 'the forms of men'. A mermaid appears on the shore, singing to the monks and promising that that evening the Abbot will sleep with her:

> For far, far down in the floors below,
> Moist as this rock-weed, cold as the snow,
> With the eel, and the clam, and the pearl of the deep,
> On soft sea-flowers [McKinnon] shall sleep,
> And long and sound shall his slumber be
> In the coral bowers of the deep with me.

The monks are not enticed by this invitation, they flee from the island in terror, and a sudden storm capsizes their boat, leaving nothing 'But a boil that arose from the deep below'. Traditional Christian images of a temple, a patriarchal God, and an underworld, are in this daring ballad strengthened and deepened by being joined to pagan, archetypal, oceanic forces.

At the end of *The Queen's Wake* come two surprising twists of irony. Queen Mary thinks Rizzio is the best minstrel, but the courtiers over-rule her decision. They choose two bards, one Highland and one Lowland, who are commanded to perform again so that the Queen may select the winner. Of course the Lowland candidate is the shepherd-poet from Ettrick. Although the Highland minstrel wins the coveted prize, Queen Mary's harp, the crafty Ettrick poet receives a second harp, older, less ornate, but of 'magic tone', which he alone recognises as the greater, more lasting, instrument. This harp will help him to subdue the storms of life and sing 'Of things below and things above', as well as giving him a power over nature, emotion, the past and the future:

> And soon corroding cares shall cease,
> And passion's host be lulled to peace;
> Angels a gilded screen shall cast,
> That cheers the future, veils the past.

At the very end of the poem comes the promise of spring and the poet's confidence in a renewal and strengthening of his creative powers. The storm remains an enemy, yet its energies have now been tamed by art, since the harp has 'taught the wandering winds to sing'. In place of the static, defiant poet of the Introduction, we now hear a poet who has learned the necessity of accepting the journey, the battle, and nature:

> Chill blows the blast around my head;
> And louder yet that blast may blow,
> When down this weary vale I've sped.

The poet is still surrounded by 'Winter's deadly hues', but he looks ahead to 'glowing suns' and 'The genial shower' in the future. Above all, James Hogg finds the symbol of the rainbow to mediate between his two antithetical image-clusters of storm and form: he will never be young again, the poet admits, yet he may still anticipate

> the rainbow's ample ring,
> That spans the glen and mountain grey,
> Though fanned by western breeze's wing,
> And sunned by summer's glowing ray.

The Queen's Wake is the first confident expression of the mature social perspectivism which dominates Hogg's work from the Spy to the Confessions and beyond. His twelve minstrels present twelve different points-of-view on the human, or Scottish, condition. Considered separately, the ballads seem 'Bold, rapid, wild, and void of art', and even each of the bards, prior to his performance, 'believed, with ready will,/ Unmatched his song, unmatched his skill', yet each part is related to the whole through careful repetitions, constrasts, and parallels. Even Queen Mary discovers this, and she enjoys the way one ballad plays 'Light as the breeze of summer-day', while others

> in solemn cadence flow,
> Smooth as the night-wind o'er the snow;
> Now bound away with rolling sweep,
> Like tempest o'er the raving deep.

There is a definite attempt by Hogg, then, to indicate that the diverse parts contribute to a unity, in the same way that different groups of people make up the Scottish nation, or for that matter the human race.

A perceptive reader may have sensed that the various journeys in *The Queen's Wake* are metaphors for the movement of consciousness, while the various battles are metaphors for decision-making. Only once is this level of meaning made explicit, when the Abbot McKinnon sets out on his fateful journey, sailing with full speed 'like an image of mind'. The journeys and battles symbolise human beings working through individual preoccupations towards an implied centre, point of unity, or ground of truth; this obscure centre is represented in different ways by Kilmeny, the monarch, and the concept of form. The 'message' of the whole poem is that truth will not be found by separate, assertive individuals, but through an appreciation of diverse temperaments, creeds, and perspectives.

Critical acclaim for *The Queen's Wake* was not long in coming. The morning after its publication the author was 'sauntering up the plainstones of the High Street', when a friendly wine merchant hailed him:

> 'Ye useless poetical deevil that ye're!' said he, 'what hae ye been doing a' this time?. . . D—n your stupid head, ye hae been pestering us wi' fourpenny papers an' daft shilly-shally sangs, an' bletherin' an' speakin' i' the Forum, an' yet had stuff in ye to produce a thing like this!' — 'Ay, Willie', said I; 'have you seen my new beuk?' — 'Ay, faith, that I have, man; and it has lickit me out o' a night's sleep. Ye hae hit the right nail on the head now. Yon's the very thing, sir'.[6]

Hogg's new friend Robert Gillies, a lawyer, author, and man of fashion in the city, heard 'a freshness, a vigour, and variety, a bold and joyous spirit in the long ballads here strung together'.[7] Gillies gave a copy to William Wordsworth, who later wrote to thank Gillies

> for the 'Queen's Wake;' since I saw you in Edinburgh I have read it. It does Mr Hogg great credit. Of the tales, I liked best, much the best, the 'Witch of Fife,' the former part of 'Kilmenie,' and the 'Abbot Mackinnon.' Mr Hogg, himself, I remember, seemed most partial to 'Mary Scott,' though he thought it too long. . . . The intermediate parts of the 'Queen's Wake' are done with much spirit, but the style here . . . is often disfigured with false finery, and in too many places it recalls Mr Scott to one's mind. Mr Hogg has too much genius to require that support, however respectable in itself.[8]

The same year brought Francis Jeffrey's first critical notice of James Hogg; Jeffrey discovered 'some traits of coarseness', and 'blemishes of diction', but concluded that 'Mr Hogg is undoubtedly a person of very considerable genius'[9] and 'worth a whole cageful of ordinary songsters from the colleges and cities of the South'.[10] The *Scots Magazine* acutely noted 'the masterly skill of the plan', as well as the 'union of the simplicity and energy of the old rhymers, with the polish of modern poetry'. An Edinburgh newspaper detected 'novelty, and . . . verisimilitude', comparing 'the plan' of Hogg's poem 'to that adopted by Boccaccio, Chaucer, and other fabulists, for the purpose of giving unity . . . to a narrative of separate . . . tales'. London's opulent *Belle Assemblée* thought *The Queen's Wake* 'worthy of admiration and indulgent criticism', while readers in Philadelphia were assured that Hogg had succeeded in 'soaring into the furthest regions of human thought'. In Boston it was said that the Ettrick Shepherd had 'listened with the ear of genius to all the breathings of passion'. Almost all the reviews were highly favourable, although one snobbish Londoner roundly denounced this 'glaring . . . violation of every principle and rule of poetry', this 'rudest barbarism', this 'dissonance, bad taste, and every fault of idle and "low-thoughted" composition'.[11] At least ten editions of the work

51

came out in the next ten years, in Edinburgh, London, Boston, Baltimore, Philadelphia, and New York. Hogg's reputation as a leading poet of the age was firmly established, with one critic stating that *The Queen's Wake* 'cannot be surpassed by any poet living or dead'.[12] But there were no profits from the early editions for James Hogg, as his publisher was made bankrupt by other investments.

Though still a poor man, the Shepherd was now a celebrity. 'Every day he was sure of being hospitably received somewhere or another at dinner', writes Gillies; 'Numberless were the convivial parties at dinner and supper' which were enlivened by Hogg's 'quaint originality of manners and inexhaustable store of good songs'. A little like Geordie Fa, James Hogg was now a natural genius who 'seemed to give himself no thought nor care about his own works, but to be engaged . . . night after night, in scraping on the fiddle, singing his own ballads, and, with the help of Glenlivat, making himself and others uproariously merry'. 'I was the first', Gillies brags,

> who brought him into repute as a welcome guest among
> what are called the upper classes of society, meaning by such
> the better and more artificially educated classes; in which
> purpose of mine the late Lady Williamson . . . aided me by
> her dinner parties. On the first of those occasions during
> dessert, the Shepherd was painfully puzzled, for not having
> till then met with ice-cream in the shape (as he said) of a
> 'fine het sweet puddin', he took, incautiously, a large spoon-
> ful, whereupon with much anxiety and tearful eyes, he
> appealed to me — 'Eh man, d'ye think that Lady Wil-
> liamson keeps ony whuskey?' to which I replied instantly,
> that I did not think but was quite certain upon that point;
> accordingly the butler, at my request, brought him a *petit
> verre*, by which he was restored to entire comfort and well-
> being.[13]

Notes

1   Gillies, *Memoirs*, II, 121.
2   Anon., 'Literary and Scientific Intelligence', *Edinburgh Quarterly Review*, Mar. 1812, p. 279.

3 Anon., 'Literary Intelligence', *Scotish Review*, Sept. 1812, p. 278.
4 Hogg, letter to Robert McTurk (Spring 1813), NLS MS 3218, f. 37.
5 Anon., 'Conversations of Maturin', *New Monthly Magazine*, May 1827, p. 409.
6 Hogg, 'Memoir', p. 26.
7 Gillies, *Memoirs*, II, 122.
8 Wordsworth, letter to Gillies, 23 Nov. 1814, printed in Gillies, *Memoirs*, II, 146.
9 Anon. rev. in *Edinburgh Review*, Nov. 1814, p. 173.
10 Anon. rev. of William Tennant's *Anster Fair*, in *Edinburgh Review*, Nov. 1814, p. 182.
11 Anon. revs. in *Scots Magazine*, Feb. 1818, p. 129; *Edinburgh Star*, 6 Feb. 1813, n.p.; *La Belle Assemblée*, Oct. 1815, p. 176; *Analectic Magazine*, Feb. 1814, p. 109; *American Monthly Magazine*, Oct. 1829, p. 530; and *Monthly Review*, Dec. 1814, p. 435.
12 J. H. (of Manchester), 'The Modern Poets: No. 1; James Hogg, the Ettrick Shepherd', *Nepenthes*, 29 Oct. 1825, p. 342.
13 Gillies, *Memoirs*, II; 129, 133, 134, 130.

Chapter Four

POETIC MIRRORS

HEROIC values and a concern for national unity made *The Queen's Wake* an ideal poem for a country at war. Yet although its 'plan proved extremely happy', Hogg could see that the *Wake* was still 'very imperfect and unequal'.[1] During 1814 and 1815, years which brought glimpses of prosperity, James Hogg wrote a series of long poems which culminated in the brilliant and witty parodies of his *Poetic Mirror*. He also revised *The Queen's Wake* to make it more saleable, modernising 'Kilmeny' and taking Scott's advice in giving a happy ending to 'The Witch of Fife'.

In 1814 Hogg was living in a rented 'den under the North Bridge', 'in an odd-looking place called St. Ann Street'.[2] The steep, dark area under the massive bridge was always 'teeming with life', and a visitor to the area would 'discover in a double sense, a lively example of what is known by the *upper* and *lower* classes'.[3] ''Twas there, up a spiral stone stair-case, in a room looking towards the Castle', John Wilson would later recall, 'that first I saw my Shepherd's honest face, and . . . ate along with him cod's head and shoulders'.[4]

These were the poet's most ambitious years. When Gillies dropped in he would find his friend 'with the old broken 'Sclate' always before him', and the slate 'covered with very close writing'.[5] The large schoolboy's relic was the same one Hogg had used many years before on the hills of Ettrick, and would keep until his final days. When writing poety, he usually worked out the lines in chalk before putting them on paper.

The summer of 1814 saw James Hogg fishing and hunting in the Highlands. A severe cold brought him to a friend's house in Athol, where, in 'a little study, furnished with books', and overlooking the beautiful River Tay, he wrote the main part of *Mador of the Moor*. *Mador* is an allegorical poem set in medieval times and lightly indebted to Spenser's *Faerie Queene*. Hogg used a modified version of the Spenserian stanza, in which each verse

54

became, for him, 'a structure of itself, resembling an arch, of which the two meeting rhymes in the middle . . . represent the key-stone, and on these all the strength and flow of the verse should rest'.[6] His rhyme-scheme, *ababcdcdd*, supposedly imitates the curling 'flow' of a river, and also gives a very different image of meaningful form through the religious or historical connotations of an 'arch' and 'key-stone'. Each verse carries a sense of process, fluidity, or flow, and a sense of eternity; the two opposite conceptions together symbolise what the poet calls a 'God of stillness and of motion', or, in other words, a spirit that is both transcendent and immanent.

Mador of the Moor begins with a vista of horror, 'Grim as the caverns in the land of death'. The King's nobles slaughter dozens of Highland roe, and then the nobles themselves are ambushed and slaughtered by their enemies. Gradually the five cantos of *Mador of the Moor* re-shape this 'dire confusion' or 'rent and formless mass' into a poet's idea of form symbolised by circles, wheels, an 'ancient ring', 'courtly ring', and fairy 'rynge', and by the union of opposites like male and female, sun and river, reason and beauty, and art and nature. The circle reconciles opposites and undermines the notion of independent categories. Disguised as Mador, a travelling minstrel, the young King makes love to Ila Moore, leaves her, and in the end marries her. The opening lines set up Hogg's basic equation between Ila (a future Queen of Scotland) and the rivers of Scotland:

> Thou Queen of Caledonia's mountain floods,
>   Theme of a thousand gifted Bards of yore,
> Majestic wanderer of the wilds and woods,
>   That lovest to circle cliff and mountain hoar.

Ila's wandering journey in search of her lover will follow three rivers in succession: the Dee, the Tay, and the Forth. While Ila represents the river, beauty, and nature, Mador represents the sun, reason, and art;

> First on the height, the beauteous morn he hail'd,
>   And rested, wondering, on the heather bell.

It seems that when Mador sleeps, his slumber is 'So deep'

> that the hand of death
> Arrests not more the reasoning faculty.

Mador of the Moor is a lively, light poem, 'now comic, now tender',[7] in the words of one disapproving critic. Responding thoughtfully and creatively to the allegorical tradition, Hogg differs from Spenser in trying to encircle or accommodate nature, rather than subduing it. He rejects the notions of courtly love and human perfectibility, turning away from 'men all pure, and maidens all divine' to paint more divided characters 'whose virtues and defects combine'. When Mador first comes to Ila's cottage, we see and hear his inept fiddling and Ila's busy-body mother and gruff father:

> The Minstrel strain'd and twisted sore his face
> > Beat with his heel, and twinkled with his eye
> But still, at every effort and grimace,
> > Louder and quicker rush'd the melody;
> > The dancers round the floor in mazes fly,
> With cheering whoop, and wheel, and caper wild
> > The jolly dame did well her mettle ply!
> Even old Kincraigy, of his spleen beguiled,
> Turn'd his dark brow aside, soften'd his looks and smiled.

Every stanza invokes Hogg's thematic symbolism of the sun and the river. Old Kincraigy is both Ila's father, and the name of a mountain near the River Dee. False love is a 'sediment', a poor poet is a 'babbler foul', Ila's childhood a 'spring . . . clouded and o'erpast', she tries to 'brook' her fears for her baby, and her love for her father is 'unbrookable'. 'Nature's own language flowed', at the end of this 'onward tale'. The river and sun together represent the poet's idea of the power, complexity, and vastness of human consciousness; when suffering 'mounts', as we hear in Canto Four, 'to o'erwhelming height',

> Oft, to itself superior, mind hath shone.
> > That broken reed, Dependence, overcome,
> Where dwells the might that may the soul unthrone,
> Whose proud resolve is moor'd on its own powers alone?

The visible universe becomes a metaphor for the creative mind, in this passage. Subtle reminders of the sun and the river — 'mounts', 'shone', 'reed', 'moor'd' — symbolise both the fertility of nature and the imagination of the poet, who loves 'amid the burning stars to sail, / Or sing with sea-maids down the coral deep'. Consciousness is able to harness the energies of nature, and can apparently redeem or humanise the chaos of life by creating significant form, which Hogg presents as a kind of cyclical journey embracing the heavens, the earth, and 'the coral deep'.

It is quite fitting that Mador seduces Ila one summer, is found by her and her baby the next summer, and promises, at the end, that although kingly duties are calling him 'to distant land', still 'next when summer flowers the highland lea / I will return, and seek my woodland home'. Like the sun, he will return each summer. The sun's upward path through the sky, and the rivers' journey through the earth down to the sea, can be seen as two halves of a whole; the two opposite journeys make up another 'ring' symbolising the cyclical rhythms of nature and the ultimate union of human, natural, and supernatural.

Edinburgh and London were pleased with the poetry, but suspicious of the subject-matter, when *Mador of the Moor* appeared in print. One reviewer heard a 'dignified simplicity' and language 'chaste, clear, and strong', but others thought that a tale of unwed pregnancy was 'not abounding in the strictest morality', or complained of Ila's being 'reduced to too low a state of humiliation', which obviously was 'not in harmony' with the proper nature of poetry. Mr Hogg's 'great error', according to the *Antijacobin*, was his habit of 'vulgar familiarity'.[8] Again and again critics insisted that only 'high' and 'proper' subjects were admissable into verse. Hogg's 1865 editor would complain that Ila, 'instead of being of a half-noble race' (as any heroine ought to be), was just 'an ordinary rural belle, a coquette, and ultimately something worse', while her lover Mador, 'in whose demeanour the dignity of royalty should appear', was sadly lacking in the necessary 'noble bearing'. Alas, then, 'What could poetry effect in behalf of such a hero and such a heroine?' As the Shepherd himself wrote, sarcastically, to a friend in England, 'you can scarcely imagine the prejudices that poverty and want of education have to encounter in this important age'.[10]

Back in Edinburgh in the autumn, James Hogg worked at his

marvellous *Pilgrims of the Sun*. This poem is truly, as one angry reader found, a work of 'insolent vaunting'.[11] Its heroine Mary Lee doubts the teachings of her medieval church and is taken on a tour of the universe by a male angel named Cela. Mary and Cela fly together as 'swift as fleets the stayless mind', beyond the elements, beyond the known universe, and beyond gravity, to where

> There was no up, there was no down,
> But all was space, and all the same.

Their journey towards the sun is a metaphor for the freedom, capacity, and 'Unspeakable delight' of enlightened, expanding consciousness.

In the second part of *Pilgrims of the Sun* the poet exchanges his native 'hill-harp' for the 'holy harp of Judah's land'. Part Second, then, slightly resembles poems like *Paradise Lost* and Edward Young's *Night Thoughts*, which Hogg sees as embodiments of a long tradition rooted in Hebraic or Biblical verse. Hogg's heaven, in contrast to Milton's, contains 'men of all creeds / Features, and hues'. Mary Lee soon transcends the limits of a 'stinted mind' which could believe

> that the Almighty's love,
> Life, and salvation, could to single sect
> Of creatures be confined, all his alike!

Nor is Paradise envisioned as a static territory set apart from process, time, or change; even in its 'ample circle',

> all were in progression — moving on
> Still to perfection. In conformity
> The human soul is modelled — hoping still
> In something onward! Something far beyond,
> It fain would grasp!

Mortal life, apparently, is only 'the infant stage / Of a progressive, endless pilgrimage'.

The third section of *Pilgrims of the Sun* uses rhyming couplets and alludes to poems by Dryden, Pope, and Johnson. Mary and

Cela are still travelling across the sky, but the worlds they now discover represent moral and social aspects of human existence. The first is a redeemed version of *The Rape of the Lock*, where ageless lovers are 'free of jealousy, their mortal bane':

> In love's delights they bask without alloy;
> The night their transport, and the day their joy.

Forever devout, constant, and wise, and beautiful, Hogg's ideal women delight in giving birth. They are no longer the victims of either hypocrisy or prudishness, since 'equal judgment' prevails between the sexes, and since the 'many faults the world heap on her head' will 'never' be reiterated here. Cela and Mary next fly to another world, a 'gloomy sphere' 'That wades in crimson'. In this world, which represents the epic poetry of Dryden and Pope, the poet concludes that a soldier is 'but an abject fool! / A king's, a tyrant's or a stateman's tool'. Indeed, Hogg is more concerned for the 'honest' and noble horses, who 'missed their generous comrades of the stall'. Yet although he dissents from Augustan attitudes towards women and towards military valour, the poet joins in their denunciation of small-minded clergymen, reviewers, and politicians: Mary and Cela

> saw the land of bedesmen discontent,
> Their frames their god, their tithes their testament!
> And snarling critics bent with aspect sour,
> T'applaud the great, and circumvent the poor;
> And knowing patriots, with important face,
> Raving aloud with gesture and grimace,
> Their prize a land's acclaim, or proud and gainful place.

Critics have been slow to understand the basic idea underlying *Pilgrims of the Sun*. Recently, however, Nelson Smith has called the poem 'thematically the most ambitious'[12] of all Hogg's works, and Douglas Gifford has joined in citing the 'strong case for reassessment'.[13] Essentially, Mary and Cela should be seen as *readers*, as they travel through literary worlds created by Milton, Dryden, Pope, and other major poets. Their literary flight is a metaphor for the Romantic imagination responding to seventeenth- and eighteenth-century English poetry. At each

59

stage of their journey Hogg adopts the appropriate style, imitating whichever poet the two pilgrims are, in effect, *reading*. James Hogg is expressing both his admiration for Milton, Dryden, Pope, and other poetic predecessors, and his sense of their limitations, since he modifies their worlds by introducing his own simpler, more natural, humanitarian and universal frame of values.

The final section of *Pilgrims of the Sun* returns the two readers to earth, where all of Ettrick Forest is in mourning for the supposed death of Mary. Her spirit watches as a monk opens her grave to steal the jewels that have been buried with her. Unable to pull the rings off her fingers, the monk takes out his knife, but as soon as it touches her flesh Mary returns to life with a shriek. This materialistic monk has of course never considered the many symbolic connotations of a 'ring' in the poems of James Hogg.

The image of a grave-robber is also used by Hogg a decade later in his *Confessions of a Justified Sinner*, where it represents finite or earthbound critics, editors, or readers. In *Pilgrims of the Sun*, like the *Confessions*, the equation between grave-robber and obtuse critic is strongly implied. And at the end of the poem we hear that the story of Mary Lee has been enjoyed 'by every Border swain' until its metaphysical lack of gravity comes under attack by pedantic commentators:

> the mass-men said, with fret and frown,
> That thro' all space it well was known,
> By moon, or stars, the earth or sea,
> An up and down there needs must be.

The 'error', 'fraud', or 'ignorance' of these Urizenic 'mass-men' imposes a literal-minded and earthbound interpretation that brings the poet back to mundane reality, just as the ring-snatching monk gravely jolts Mary back to her senses and back to the world of gravity she had left behind.

During their travels Mary's and Cela's 'frame and vision' are 'subtilised' so that they can appreciate 'the inner regions' which they explore. The main feature of their expanded awareness is its passivity or receptiveness, its freedon from aggressive intellect, and from dogma, theory, or preconception. Their flight (or, in other words, their thinking) is rapid, effortless, and smooth, as they glide through vast realms,

> Bent forward on the wind, in graceful guise,
> On which they seemed to press, for their fair robes
> Were streaming far behind them.

> So swift and so untroubled was their flight,
> 'Twas like the journey of a dream by night.

'[L]eaning forward on the liquid air, / Like twin-born eagles', the travellers learn to trust the natural and divine power that impels them. Their flight becomes, suggestively, 'an arch', 'Formed like the rainbow', 'Circling the pales of heaven'. Normally subjectivity is set against the objective, physical world, but now subjective and objective are continually merging through the fluidity of process. As Mary looks around she sees that

> the stars and the moon fled west away,
> So swift o'er vaulted sky they shone;
> They seemed like fiery rainbows reared,
> In a moment seen, in a moment gone.

A major contribution to Romantic poetry is contained in these passages, with their profound sense of motion foreshadowing the fantastic chariots of Shelley, Byron, and Poe. Mary and Cela are in a kind of 'rapid chariot' moving 'thro' mind's unwearied range'. 'O let us onward steer', cries Mary, 'The light our steeds, the wind our charioteer'. Her experience of process teaches Mary to see 'a God in all', whom 'All Nature worshipped', and to whom even the flowers give 'unconscious Worship'. The pantheistic undertones, the union of male and female, the metaphor of flight, the Faustian confidence in the power of the human mind, and the implied analogy between artistic creation and divine creation, all indicate a strong Romantic influence in *Pilgrims of the Sun*, which, according to one critic, 'Lord Byron in his Cain, and Shelley in his Queen Mab, have palpably imitated'.[14]

Pilgrims of the Sun was apparently too daring for any of the Edinburgh publishers, but it greatly impressed John Murray, Byron's London publisher, who offered £500 for the manuscript and the copyright. Hogg preferred to accept £80 and retain the rights, since he hoped to produce his collected poems in the future. However, Murray had second thoughts, and a letter from the Shepherd, written the day after Christmas in 1814, begins, 'Dear Murray, What the deuce have you made of my excellent poem that you are never publishing it while I am starving for want of money and cannot even afford a Christmas goose to my friends?'[15] When it finally appeared, the critics were sharply divided. *The Scots Magazine* was 'best pleased' with those parts 'in which [the author] has not quite lost sight of his native earth'. A Boston critic found *Pilgrims of the Sun* 'the most original of his works', yet advised Hogg to give up writing, since 'There seem . . . to be insurmountable difficulties in the way of his being a powerful or a popular writer'. A Shrewsbury reviewer could 'say without hesitation, that it displays so great a share of 'heaven born genius', as to assure it an immortality', and in London Hogg was heralded as 'the rival or the compeer of Southey and of Wordsworth, of Byron and of Campbell'. *The Augustan Review* detected 'very considerable merit':

> The author is said, at one time or another, to have been a shepherd; and, as such, to possess little learning. Granted that he is not classical; but neither is he unlearned — if to have read and understood, as it is obvious Mr Hogg has done, most of the best books in our own language can raise a man above the imputation of being destitute of learning.[16]

In his autobiography James Hogg recalls that he first intended his *Pilgrims of the Sun* as part of 'a volume of romantic poems, to be entitled "Midsummer Night Dreams"'. Unfortunately a friend convinced him to publish the three parts separately, an arrangement he grew to regret: 'Among other wild and visionary subjects, the 'Pilgrims of the Sun' would have done very well, and might at least have been judged one of the best; but, as an entire poem by itself, it bears an impress of extravagance, and affords no relief from the story of a visionary existence'.[17]

The second poem intended for *Midsummer Night Dreams* was 'Connel of Dee', a comic ballad which complements *Pilgrims of the Sun* in the way that 'The Witch of Fife' complements 'Kilmeny'. The hero, Connel, is the opposite of Mary Lee in every respect. Licentious, libidinous, dissatisfied, and impious, he is taken by a wordly 'young maiden'[18] to her castle, where they marry and live happily, at least until Connel discovers 'in his bosom a fathomless void, / A yearning again to be free'.

Mary Lee's daytime journey had been one of freedom, an ascent through the sky, heaven, and poetry. But Connel's night journey is one of enslavement, a descent through a depraved, materialistic society into the purely physical and the element of water. Connel soon tires of his wife's aristocratic connections,

> A race whom he hated, a profligate breed,
> The scum of existence to vengeance decreed!
> Who laughed at their God and their friend.

He complains of his wife's infidelity, but she merely laughs,

> Why that was the fashion! — no sensible man
> Could e'er of such freedom complain,

clamping a hand on his mouth and introducing him to a few unpleasant facts:

> Peace booby! if life thou regardest beware,
> I have had some fair husbands ere now;
> They wooed, and they flattered, they sighed and they sware,
> At length they grew irksome like you.

In the gruesomely comic scene that follows Connel meets his wife's ex-husband, who is chained in a dungeon above a trap-door. The trap-door opens, and the terrified man is beheaded by a pair of mechanical shears. Connel, horrified, flees from the castle to the river; 'he skimmed the wild paths like a thing of the mind'.

> It may not be said that he ran, for he flew,
> Straight on for the hills of the Dee.

Connel's hectic flight from his 'vision of death' is a parody of Mary Lee's orderly, smooth, and joyous journey:

Thro' gallwood and bramble he floundered amain,
    No bar his advancement could stay;
Tho' heels-o'er-head whirled again and again,
    Still faster he gained on his way.
This moment on swinging bough powerless he lay,
    The next he was flying along;
So lightly he scarce made the green leaf to quake,
Impetuous he splashed thro' the bog and the lake,
He rainbowed the hawthorn, he needled the brake,
    With power supernaturally strong.

At last he comes to the Loch of Dee. Still pursued by his wife,
'Well mounted, with devilish speed', Connel dives into the water
and drowns, yet his mind survives 'All passive':

He died, but he found that he never would be
    So dead to all feeling and smart,
No, not though his flesh were consumed in the Dee,
    But that eels would some horror impart.

Just when the rude eels have 'warped all his bowels about on the
tide', Connel hears his wife calling him. He gathers up his
intestines and flees in dismay, only to find that everything has
been a dream. His journey has taken him from initial pride and
self-sufficiency down to a physical realm of material possession
and sexual promiscuity, followed by a further descent into a
watery, amorphous element which signifies the unconscious, the
fragility of the self, and death. But the ending restores Connel to
tranquillity and happiness, when he learns (like Coleridge's
Ancient Mariner) to share his experience of the journey with
others:

And oft on the shelve of the rock he reclined,
    Light carolling humoursome rhyme,
Of his midsummer dream, of his feelings refined,
    Or some song of the good olden time.
And even in age was his spirit in prime.
    Still reverenced on Dee is his name!
His wishes were few, his enjoyments were rife,
He loved and he cherished each thing that had life,
With two small exceptions, an eel and a wife,
    Whose commerce he dreaded the same.

'Connel of Dee' is an extended metaphor to describe the poet's descent into the unconscious. It perfectly mirrors the ascent of the conscious mind in *Pilgrims of the Sun*. Taken together, the two main poems of *Midsummer Night Dreams* form a ring or cycle, just as the two types of journey in *Mador of the Moor* form a ring that symbolically encircles and unites opposite aspects of human life.

In the years surrounding Waterloo James Hogg was a highly unorthodox and free-wheeling visionary whose best poems try to find universal values and try to relate those values to the Scottish, British, and Christian world in which he lived. His series of *Sacred Melodies* is set to hymns taken from German synagogues, and follows the story of Israel from past bondage to future freedom, when 'The happy child'[19] 'Shall frolic with delight' and 'All in love unite'. Perhaps Hogg's most shocking poem is 'Superstition', which was intended as a third and final part of *Midsummer Night Dreams*. This short piece defends ancient Scottish witchcraft and condemns the present conformist and rationalistic 'cold saturnine morn'.[20] The poet admits that 'every creed has its attendant ills', but claims that the days of witches

> were the times for holiness of frame;
> Those were the days when fancy wandered free;
> That kindled in the soul the mystic flame,
> And the rapt breathings of high poesy.

'Superstition' argues for a continuity of Christian and pre-Christian beliefs. By separating modern religion from its primitive roots, the poet warns, the present age was unintentionally obliterating the basis of faith, which now

> In the eye of reason wears into decline;
> And soon that heavenly ray must ever cease to shine.

It was about this time that James Hogg began to work on his *Queen Hynde*, 'an epic poem on a regular plan' which he believed would turn out to be his 'greatest work'.[21] *Queen Hynde* is truly an epic, with its grand scale, its historical battles and journeys, its theme of the founding of a nation, its use of gods, legend, and history, and its confident narrative tone which allows the chronicler both to comment on the moral significance of events, and to draw important parallels with modern life. A fictitious tale based loosely on historical facts, *Queen Hynde* is Hogg's vision of the freeing of Scotland from Viking domination many centuries before. In addition to this main plot, the work discusses the relation of dreams to reality, the superceding of 'primitive' religion by Christianity, and above all the nature of Hogg's Edinburgh audience.

The poet draws quiet parallels between the divisions and limitations of medieval Scotland, and analogous follies which he finds in the readers of his own age. At the start of her reign the beautiful young Hynde is uncertain, inexperienced, and too much the prey of her emotions. These qualities are echoed in the sentimental women readers of Hogg's time, as we understand when the narrator repeatedly breaks in with sarcastic cries of frustration:

> Maids of Dunedin, in despair   Edinburgh
> Will ye not weep and rend your hair?
> Ye who, in these o'erpolish'd times,
> Can shed the tear o'er woful rhymes;
> O'er plot of novel sore repine,
> And cry for hapless heroine —
> . . .
> If in such breast a heart may be,
> Sure you must weep and wail with me!

Again and again through the long middle section of *Queen Hynde* the poet gleefully flings his insults at his fashionable, genteel women readers:

> And well 'tis known that woman's mind
> Is still to noise and stir inclined;
> She would be mark'd, and woo'd withal,
> Rather to ill than not at all.

These comments, however, should be seen with some appreciation of their irony and their place in the poem as a whole. The poet's alienation from his audience is an appropriate and subtle mirror to the division existing in medieval Scotland as depicted in the scenes of political intrigue and battle. As the poet says to his readers at the beginning of the fifth section, 'The song is a medley, and model of thee'. It is very fitting, therefore, that when Queen Hynde is forced into exile and the Vikings over-run Scotland, the poet concedes that he has probably offended most of his audience:

> Fair maid of Albyn's latter day,
> How brook'st thou now thy shepherd's lay?
> . . .
> Full sorely art thou cross'd, I ween,
> In what thou wished'st to have seen;
> The amends lies not within my power,
> But in thine own, beloved flower!

In other words the reader can understand this poem if she or he will try to find significant themes rather than reading with 'burning thirst' in a headlong, sentimental, or literal fashion that only seeks 'To shed the tear and rue the deed'. 'Be this thy lesson', says the narrator simply; 'pause, and think'.

The end of Book Fifth is the lowest point in the action of *Queen Hynde*. It marks the complete victory of the Vikings, the flight of the Scottish court, and the death of thousands of Scots in battle. Once again Hogg brings together the two main strands of his epic, by choosing this moment to banish certain groups of his audience. The immature readers he sends into exile include those who

> without waiting to contend,
> Begin the book at the wrong end,
> And read it backward! By his crook,
> This is a mode he will not brook!

> Next, he debars all those who sew
> Their faith unto some stale review;
> That ulcer of our mental store,
> The very dregs of manly lore;
> Bald, brangling, brutal, insincere;
> The bookman's venal gazetteer;
> Down with the trash, and every gull
> That gloats upon their garbage dull!

He next debars (God save the mark!)
All those who read when it is dark,
Boastful of eyesight, harping on,
Page after page in maukish tone,
And roll the flowing words off hand,
Yet neither feel nor understand;
All those who read and doze by day,
To while the weary time away!

. . .

He next debars all those who dare,
Whether with proud and pompous air,
With simpering frown, or nose elate,
To name the word INDELICATE!

Having exiled those readers who approach his epic in a
trivialising, narrow, or unsympathetic manner, the poet makes
peace with his Edinburgh 'darlings' and tells them (— a little like
Hynde trying to inspire her soldiers —) that 'We must now
pursue / Our theme, for we have much to do'. He also begins to
lay aside his resentment of his audience:

Oft hast thou grieved his heart full sore
With thy sly chat and flippant lore;
Thy emphasis on error small,
And smile, more cutting far than all;
The praise, half compliment, half mock,
The minstrel's name itself a joke!
But yet, for all thy airs and whims,
And lightsome lore the froth that skims,
He must acknowledge in the end
To 've found thee still the poet's friend,
His friend at heart.

The way is now clear for a reconciliation between the artist and
his women readers, those 'dear maids of Scotia wide', and also for
a resurrection and re-unification of Scotland. But these happy
consummations are darkened by a surprise event so sudden, cruel,
and shocking that even the poet loses his epic tone for a moment:

68

Well might they say, on such a lot,
Is there a God in heaven or not?

Queen Hynde was not published until the end of 1824, nearly a decade after much of it was written. The critics failed to share Hogg's high opinion of his work. Almost unanimously the reviewers decreed that *Queen Hynde* was 'destitute of elegance', contained 'low and vulgar images', and showed only 'raving dulness'. Despite a Londoner's praise for 'This wildly beautiful and very original poem', and the *Edinburgh Observer*'s perceptive comments on Hogg's 'forcible and homely language', 'his very disregard of [false] style, and abhorrence of fastidious delicacy', most critics were horrified to discover 'a sad tampering with sacred themes' which seemed to verge on 'absolute blasphemy'. An Ayrshire reader pointed out 'all the vulgarity — all the bad rhymes — all the coarseness — all the indecencies — and all the gross egotism', adding snobbishly that 'the sheep-shearer's *vulgar* style' was what 'we might expect to be favoured with when Jamie Hogg attempts to compose an epic poem'. 'We decline sullying our pages with such offensive matter', declared the *Critical Gazette*, which was 'convinced that to a well regulated mind many passages in Queen Hynde would be considered more reprehensible than any thing to be found in [Shelley's] Queen Mab'.[22]

James Hogg never met Shelley, but he became acquainted with many other leading writers of the day. He first met William and Mary Wordsworth at an Edinburgh dinner-party in 1814. Though surprised at the Englishman's appearance — 'grey russet jacket and pantaloons' and a 'broad-brimmed beaver hat' — the Shepherd was proud to go with his new friends along the River Yarrow: 'We went into my father's cot, and partook of some homely refreshment, visited St. Mary's Lake, which that day was calm, and pure as any mirror; and Mrs. Wordsworth in particular testified great delight with the whole scene'.[23] Later that year Hogg rode with John Wilson down to the English lake district, where he was entertained for a few weeks by the Wordsworths, Robert Southey, Thomas De Quincey, and others.

Byron used his connections to help Hogg, and the two men enjoyed reading each other's poetry. 'Hogg is a strange being', wrote Byron, 'but of great, though uncouth, powers. I think very highly of him as a poet'.[24] Byron's letters to the Shepherd are robust, hastily-written, and slightly condescending: 'And so —

you want to come to London — it is a damned place — to be sure — but the only one in the world — (at least in the English world) for fun'.[25]

James Hogg wanted his literary friends to help him financially by writing for a collection of verse which he planned to edit. Although Byron and Wordsworth promised to send poems, they later changed their minds. At this time Hogg was quarrelling violently with Scott, and he began to see that no major writers would support his new venture. His very ambivalent feelings towards Byron, Wordsworth, Coleridge, Southey and Wilson are beautifully portrayed in his *Poetic Mirror*, which he decided, with unusual prudence, to publish anonymously.

Like Mr Shuffleton of *The Spy*, James Hogg once again holds up a mirror to show his contemporary poets in their true colours. The first satire of his *Poetic Mirror* is 'The Guerilla', an exaggerated version of Byron's medieval horror-poems. The 'hot and restless' hero, Alayni, will tolerate 'No rival nor superior'. He leads his Spanish villagers on a raid of vengeance after his lover Kela has been captured and dishonoured by Gauls. After slaughtering his enemies, the bloodthirsty Alayni then murders Kela as well, since she has become 'a lothful stain'. He then proposes to sacrifice his female captives, but instead his warriors merely debauch them. Still fixated by past events, Alayni visits each tent after nightfall, butchering the women and ripping out the heart of the one warrior who opposes his violence.

Alayni resembles Macgregor of *The Queen's Wake*: his 'mind would better suit the raving storm'. A victim of the past and the purely physical, he ignores conscience and has no redeeming sense of form:

> But that insatiate yearning of the mind
> Still preying, hungering, craving still to prey,
> Doom'd never bourn or resting-place to find;
> O that must torture, undivulged for aye,
> Save in the soul's still voice, the eye's perturbed ray!

Alayni's 'insatiate yearning' is Hogg's metaphor for the Byronic temperament. Byron, then, is unfree, insensitive, unfair to women, inhumane, and heartless.

In his next parody, 'Wat o' the Cleuch', Hogg makes fun of the typical characters, situations, and comforting moral resolutions of

70

Walter Scott's historical poems. Wat is a kind of Scottish Alayni, a terror to friend and foe alike. Disguised as a monk in order to recapture Roxburgh Castle, Wat is offended when the Abbot at Roxburgh denounces in prayer a certain hot-headed warrior:

> A thief he is and coward too,
> God's adversary, Wat o' the Cleuch.

The gigantic Wat immediately forgets his disguise, leaning forward 'with his nostrils breathing ire' to whisper in the Abbot's ear,

> Thou dunghill mass of corruptness!
> What devil in hell hath told thee this?

Once he gets inside the castle, the hero hears himself ridiculed by a common minstrel; the minstrel claims that when

> Wat o' the Cleuch kneel'd down to pray,
> He wist not what to do or say;
> But he pray'd for beef, and he pray'd for bree,   soup
> A two-hand spoon and a haggies to pree.   haggis to taste

Wat instantly throws off his monk's cowl and begins slicing up his detractors. The poem ends merrily with his improbable victory over a whole army of mere Englishmen:

> Off went the Southron heads like hail!
> Not one by one, nor two by two,
> But in whole files he laid them low.

Walter Scott's materialism, credulity, patriotism, and predictability are brought to light in these lines. Scott and Byron may be opposites in many ways, but Hogg is suggesting that they are both possessed by the past and by physical reality.

The funniest parts of *The Poetic Mirror* are three parodies of Wordsworth's unfinished poem, *The Recluse*. In the first, 'The Stranger', Hogg points out Wordsworth's visual obsession, his mundane realism, and his extravagant, prosaic moralising. A traveller —

> Red was the corner of his eye, and yet
> It seem'd to beam a glance of living flame

— comes to a 'peaceful solitary lake' where he simply wanders into the water and drowns. Later 'Wordsworth' leads his fellow-poets James Hogg, Robert Southey, and John Wilson to the spot, shows them the man's skeleton, and launches into a ponderous dissertation on human nature:

'There lies the channel, and original bed,'
Continued I, still pointing to the lake,
'From the beginning hollow'd out and scoop'd
For man's affections, else betray'd and lost,
And swallow'd up 'mid desarts infinite.
This is the genuine course, the aim and end
Of prescient reason, all conclusions else
Are abject, vain, presumptuous, and perverse.'

Like his traveller, 'Wordsworth' becomes enthralled by the lake, but instead of drowning he stands transfixed at the shore, hypnotised by a portentous shape he sees moving under the water:

More had I said, resuming the discourse
. . .
But that, chancing again to turn my eyes
Toward the bosom of that peaceful mere,
I saw a form so ominous approach
My heart was chill'd with horror — through the wave
Slowly it came — by heaven I saw it move
Toward the grizly skeleton! . . .
At sight of such a hideous messenger,
Thus journeying through the bowels of the deep,
O'er sluggish leaf and unelaborate stone,
All Nature stood in mute astonishment,
As if her pulse lay still — onward it came,
And hovering o'er the bones, it linger'd there
In a most holy and impressive guise.
I saw it shake its hideous form, and move
Towards my feet — the elements were hush'd,
The birds forsook their singing, for the sight
Was fraught with wonder and astonishment.
It was a tadpole — somewhere by itself
The creature had been left, and there had come
Most timeously, by Providence sent forth,
To close this solemn and momentous tale.

72

If 'The Stranger' suggests that Wordsworth's vision is essentially static, 'The Flying Tailor' takes the opposite approach, attacking the English poet's capacity for far-fetched comparisons through the metaphor of a 'Frog-like' apprentice able to jump long distances 'o'er the many-headed multitude'. There is such a 'Rare correspondence, wondrous unity' between the tailor's 'bodily and mental form', that, just as he is a great jumper in the physical sense, so he can also leap, in his thinking, between physical and spiritual, since he possesses 'the power intuitive / Of diving into character', thereby finding 'many a mystic notch' merely from plying his trade as a tailor:

> A pair
> Of breeches to his philosophic eye
> Were not what unto other folks they seem,
> Mere simple breeches, but in them he saw
> The symbol of the soul — mysterious, high
> Hieroglyphics! such as Egypt's Priest
> Adored upon the holy Pyramid,
> Vainly imagined tomb of monarchs old,
> But raised by wise philosophy, that sought
> By darkness to illumine, and to spread
> Knowledge by dim concealment — process high
> Of man's imaginative, deathless soul.

Unrestrained by common sense, the frog-like 'Wordsworth' makes giant leaps, in this passage, from a pair of pants to ancient Egypt to Milton to eternal life.

In 'James Rigg', the next parody, Hogg finds Wordsworth fundamentally blind (despite his preoccupation with vision) and solipsistic. James Rigg is a quarry worker who accidentally blinds himself when his dynamite goes off prematurely. Rigg is so slow-witted and ponderous that it takes him several minutes to understand what has happened:

> He stood awhile,
> Wondering from whence that tumult might proceed,
> And all unconscious that the blast had dimm'd
> His eyes for ever, and their smiling blue
> Converted to a pale and mournful grey.

F

Was it, he thought, some blast the quarrymen
Blasted at Conniston, or in that vale,
Call'd from its huge and venerable yew,
Yewdale? (though other etymologists
Derive that appellation from the sheep,
Of which the female in our English tongue
Still bears the name of ewe.)
. . . Or had news arrived
Of Buonaparte's last discomfiture . . . ?
It next perhaps occurr'd to him to ask,
Himself, or some one near him, if the sound
Was not much louder than those other sounds,
Fondly imagined by him, — and both he,
And that one near him, instantly replied
Unto himself, that most assuredly
The noise proceeded from the very stone,
Which they two had so long been occupied
In boring, and that probably some spark,
Struck from the gavelock 'gainst the treacherous flint,
Had fallen amid the powder, and so caused
The stone t'explode, as gunpowder will do,
With most miraculous force, especially
When close ramm'd down into a narrow bore,
And cover'd o'er with a thin layer of sand
To exclude the air; else otherwise. . . .

Here James Hogg is of course hitting off Wordsworth's long-windedness, his difficulties in distinguishing between self and other, the scarcity of 'sparks' of wit in his poems, and above all his most *'boring'* work, *The Recluse.* We are consoled at the end with the news that Rigg, though mildly upset at being blind, learns to compensate with his remaining senses, since 'gracious Nature' feeds the soul with images 'even as if th' external world / Were the great wet-nurse of the human race'. Wordsworth, according to the Shepherd, is a captive of his own personal past, his infancy.

With 'Isabelle' and 'The Cherub' Hogg turns to ridiculing the obscure mysticism and portentous numerology of Coleridge. Neither poem makes any attempt to clarify the dimness, the first simply ending with the poet's enigmatic cry,

The hour's at hand, O woe is me!
For they are coming, and they are three!

and the second implying that the poet is just as confused as his
reader:

The happy vision is no more!
But in its room a darker shade
Than eye hath pierced, or darkness made;
I cannot turn, yet do not know,
What I would, or whither go.

As one critic observed, Hogg has captured 'The soft *unmeaning-
ness* of what Mr. Coleridge terms a conclusion'.[26]

'Peter of Barnet' is a brilliant send-up of the poet laureate
Robert Southey's experiments in metre and ballad techniques.
After hearing Burns's poem, 'To a Mountain-Daisy, On turning
one down, with the Plough', the cantankerous and pompous bard
rushes out to his fields to find a daisy and instruct his ploughman
not to overturn it:

He took a stone,
And placed it tall on end. — Herbert, said he,
When thou plough'st down this ridge, spare me this flower.
I charge thee note it well, — and for thy life
Do it no injury. — Pugh! said the clown,
Such stuff! — I shall not mind it — He went on
Whistling his tune — Oh Peter was most wroth!
He ran in hasty guise around, and looked
For a convenient stone, that he might throw
And smite the ploughman's head. — No one would suit.
Then, turning round to me, he gave full vent
To's rage against the hind, and all was o'er.
In his first heat, he cursed the menial race;
I told you they were all alike, said he,
A most provoking and ungracious set. . . .

This passage contrasts a sentimental attitude towards nature and
the lower classes with the reality of Southey's official Toryism. It
also captures Southey's heavy-handed attempts to emulate Burns,

whom he greatly admired. The two sides, pretense and reality, are pointedly symbolised in the poet's two uses — equally ineffective — for stones. A ploughman himself, Burns would have been one of that 'most provoking and ungracious set' which this bard curses roundly; and in Burns's poem it is Burns himself, as ploughman, who speaks to the daisy after turning it under.

The other parody of Southey is the aptly-titled 'Curse of the Laureate'. The laureate is engaged in 'happy slumbering', dreaming of his literary progeny as they parade before him, when suddenly the celebration is interrupted with the appearance of Francis Jeffrey, a foolish fiend who unaccountably denounces Southey's poems. A friendlier spirit then appears, whispering to 'Southey' that his name will last forever, 'To Milton and to Spenser next in fame'. As the poem ends 'Southey' is pronouncing his long 'awful curse of destiny' against the critic Jeffrey. Hogg's target in 'Curse of the Laureate' is Southey's *Curse of Kehama*, in which the god Kehama, a proud, tyrannical ruler of the world and of heaven, condemns his enemy to eternal torment; the implication is that Southey resembles Kehama, and that like Kehama the laureate will fall from power and favour after uttering his curse.

Three brief imitations of Hogg's new friend John Wilson conclude *The Poetic Mirror*. With scathing irony, these pieces capture the disembodied and saccharine qualities of Wilson's *Isle of Palms*. The 'Hymn to the Moon' ends with the distraught 'Wilson' abandoned in darkness by his muse:

> Where art thou gone? all of a sudden gone?
> Why hast thou left thy pensive worshipper
> Sitting in the darkness on the mossy stump
> Of an old oak-tree?

Deserted by his imagination, 'Wilson' has soon become pedantic and self-important.

The seventh of fourteen pieces in *The Poetic Mirror* is 'The Gude Greye Katt', Hogg's self-mocking parody of his 'Witch of Fife' and 'Kilmeny'. The poet makes fun of his own antiquarian ballad style and his use of fantastic situations, shifting personal identities, and far-fetched metaphors and allegories. The Lairde of Blain has no wife, seven daughters, and a talking cat. His remarkably gifted cat, who is also a beautiful woman, and also the Queen of the Fairies, is examined by an evil, self-serving bishop on a charge of witchcraft. The cat then collars the bishop and carries him through the roof and up across the sky:

> The braide ful mone wase up the lyft,   broad full moon
> The nychte wase lyke ane daye,   night
> As the greate Byschope tuke his jante
> Up throu the milkye-waye.

To his chagrin the bishop is dropped into the volcanic Mount Etna, while the cat continues on her flight. Meanwhile on earth the laird's seven daughters have perished, but by the end of the poem they are dipped in 'the krystal streime' and given eternal life.

The symbolism of 'The Gude Greye Katt' can be understood in the context of earlier works such as 'Mr Shuffleton's Allegorical Survey', 'Story of Two Highlanders'. and *Midsummer Night Dreams*. The cat unites human, natural, and supernatural qualities, and represents the imagination of James Hogg. Rational consciousness, whether of Hogg himself or of his readers or critics, is represented by the unfortunate bishop, who can only go part-way on the cat's journey, and is fittingly deposited in Mount Etna, a symbol of literary orthodoxy. The Lairde of Blain is probably James Hogg in his ordinary, public, Edinburgh or Ettrick personality; his seven daughters would then correspond to Hogg's seven books of poetry, for which he is predicting eternal life, even though they may have 'died' for the present.

'The Gude Greye Katt' is the only poem in *The Poetic Mirror* to present in full Hogg's version of a symbolic journey of ascent. Flying between the earth and heaven, the complex and gifted cat traces an arc which supposedly reconciles natural, human, supernatural and divine, as well as past (in this case, fifteenth-century Scotland) with present and future. The cat's song as she sweeps across the milky way is so alluring that it brings about a reunion and rejuvenation of nature on earth, with all the animals dancing in rings:

> The Murecokis dancit ane seuinsum ryng   Moorcocks danced
> Arunde the hether bell;

77

The Foumartis jyggit by the brukis,   Polecats jigged
The Maukinis by the kaile,   Hares; cabbage
And the Otar dancit ane minowaye   minuet
As he gaed ouir the daile.

The cat's journey is mainly an ascent, but the other half, the descending journey, is present through the bishop's fall into the black crater, which is also Hell. The full circuit of ascent and descent would make another 'ryng', with each half being a mirror-image of the other, as the words of cat and bishop ironically imply:

He cryit, O Pussie, hald your gryp,
  O hald and dinna spaire;
O drap me in the yerde or se,   earth or sea
  But dinna drap me there.   i.e., in the volcano

But scho wase ane doure and deidlye katt,   she was
  And scho saide with lychtsum ayre,
You kno heuin is ane blissit plece,   heaven
  And all the prestis gang there.   priests

Och sweete, sweete Pussye, hald your gryp,
  Spaire nouther cleke nor clawe.
Is euir that lyke heuin abone,   above
  In quhich am lyke to fa'?   I'm like to fall?

As in *The Queen's Wake*, then, the central poem in *The Poetic Mirror* provides a standard to help us in understanding the other constituent poems. Hogg is admitting and ridiculing his own egotism, while also insinuating that only *his* poems achieve a full sense of human freedom, movement, and potential. The singing, flying cat has a vitality and wholeness of vision which is sadly lacking, according to James Hogg, in most of the other poets of the day. We hear the cramped, static quality of those other poets in 'Wordsworth's' tell-tale allusion to 'the unvoyageable sky', in 'Coleridge's' admission that he 'cannot turn' and doesn't know 'What I would, or whither go', and in 'Southey's' fatuous reaction on hearing of the persecution suffered by Burns:

78

> D—n them! said Peter, — he thrust back his chair,
> Dashed one knee o'er the other furiously,
> Took snuff a double portion, — swallowed down
> His glass at once, — look'd all around the room
> With wrathful eye, and then took snuff again.

At the opposite extreme from these stuffy poets is 'Byron', whose hero Alayni ends in a frenzy of futile exertion, 'in maniac guise 'mid bloody broil'. The poet in 'Wat o' the Cleuch' may think that his verse is as 'Free as the summer's cloudless breeze', but the reality of Scott's repetitive, monotonous poety is more accurately captured in a description of Wat in battle:

> With madden'd motion, quite the same
> As if his tall gigantic frame
> Had been machine, that battle knell
> Could set, and keep in movement well.

Whether the bards themselves are static or engaged in a frenzy of motion, Byron, Scott, Wordsworth, Coleridge and Southey are each shown to depict journeys of despair, futile descents into the historical or personal past, or into a purely physical realm represented by battles, lakes, a tadpole or frog, obscurity, darkness, a daisy, or a rock. Only John Wilson is allowed an ascent, and in 'The Morning Star' the star's movement through the sky is Hogg's tribute to his friend's poetry, which allegedly moves

> Calm onward without breeze or tide,
> With stedfast and unaltered motion,
> Along the bright and starry ocean.

But like the other parodies of Wilson this one ends on a note of abandonment and confusion, with the star's disappearance and the forlorn poet deserted by imagination and 'look[ing] in vain'. With the exception of 'The Gude Greye Katt', each section of *The Poetic Mirror* describes a partial journey, a voyage downward or upward which terminates at the lowest or highest point, apparently because the poets are incapable of drawing the symbolic, universal, or social implications which would permit a return to everyday life and a useful communication to others of the experience of the journey.

James Hogg was a genuine Romantic poet, a creator of metaphors and myth to embody difficult truths. The cosmic cycles or rings of his greatest poems convey a wholeness which, as *The Poetic Mirror* indicates, is intended to preserve the free imagination from a reductive skepticism like that of Byron, and equally from the too-idealistic, saccharine tone of John Wilson's poetry. Other poets may present incomplete segments of descent or ascent, but Hogg tries to draw the full circle of human experience, to reconcile such opposites as reason and instinct, conscious and unconscious, objective and subjective, physical and spiritual, despair and joy, or comic and tragic.

In the mature myth-making of *Mador, Midsummer Night Dreams*, and *The Poetic Mirror*, the Shepherd develops images and motifs which were present from his very first poems. The watery element has now become the three rivers in *Mador*, the Loch of Dee in *Midsummer Night Dreams*, and the obsession of the 'lake poets' in *The Poetic Mirror*. Each work describes a downward journey into this chaotic realm, followed by a return to community. In these long poems, however, the parabola of descent is coupled with its mirror-image of an ascending journey into knowledge or imagination, as represented by the course of the sun or by the flights of Mary Lee or the good grey cat. A similar mirror-effect can be found in *Queen Hynde*, with its military unification of Scotland, on one hand, and reconciliation between the poet and his readers, on the other.

Like most of Hogg's best work, the major poems begin with self-confident protagonists who are separated from normal humanity by virtue of rank (like Mador and Queen Hynde), extreme suffering or exile (Ila Moore and Hynde), intelligence or skepticism (Mary Lee), discontent (Connel of Dee), or the pompous pretensions to profundity by the various poets in *The Poetic Mirror*. Each individualistic self then traces either the upper path of reason, imagination, or spirituality, or the lower path which leads to despair, defeat in battle, the unconscious, or physical nature. The parallels between the two journeys are most clearly shown in *Midsummer Night Dreams*, with Mary Lee experiencing a *joyous* disintegration of selfhood through her sensitive reading of poetry, and Connel experiencing a *despairing* disintegration of selfhood through his encounter with the purely physical, the nightmare, and the eels. However divergent the two paths may be, they converge at the end in a vision of redeemed community, social usefulness and harmony, and an implied notion of a more authentic self which has learned to accept its own relativity, its dependence upon society, nature, love, and process.

In January 1815 James Hogg was granted the rent-free possession of a small farm on Altrive Lake, in his native Ettrick Forest, as a gift from the Duke of Buccleuch. The farm was then stocked with sheep, labourers were hired to do much of the work, and Hogg was free to divide his time between country and city. His summers could now be spent fishing for 'bull-trout, singing songs, and drinking whisky'.[27] A fisherman who travelled through Ettrick in June 1815 records that he 'surprised [Hogg] in his cottage bottling whisky'.[28]

On his visits to the capital, the Shepherd would lodge either with the newly-wed Gillies, or at Teviot Row, under the roof of John Grieve, a hat-maker and amateur poet. Here at Grieve's, 'as business every day called his host abroad, he had the entire house to himself, with store of books and music, from the breakfast hour till dinner time'. Gillies says that this period 'was about the happiest' of his friend's life. For the Edinburgh evenings Hogg 'planned music-parties after his own fancy'; these were jubilant affairs at which the poet sang, played the fiddle, danced, and got devoutly intoxicated. His future wife Margaret Phillips probably attended, as did the wealthy Mrs. Brooke Richmond, a 'horse-woman and fox huntress' who 'delighted in promoting the hilarity of social circles'. A word 'from *her* voice', says Gillies, 'would at any time rouse the Shepherd to sing the most uproarious of his festive songs'.[29] Another guest at these parties recalls drinking French wine 'till ten o'clock, at which hour we transferred ourselves to the drawing-room, and began dancing reels in a most clamorous and joyous manner, to the music sometimes of the Shepherd's fiddle — sometimes of the harpsichord'.[30]

Meanwhile the farm at Altrive was becoming a financial strain, especially with an economic depression getting under way in 1816. As the storm worsened Hogg wrote less verse and turned to the short stories and novels which would appeal to a wider, more dependable, less educated market. For the rest of his life most of his income came from short pieces written for *Blackwood's* and other periodicals. The new audience wanted gossip, personality, and humour, at the expense of imagination, ideas, and wit, yet paradoxically the fiction of his last two decades is James Hogg's greatest artistic achievement.

Hogg was a prolific writer, and only the brevity of this study prevents consideration of his vast number of songs, his verse dramas (which were published but never performed), his masque and anti-masque for the coronation of George the Fourth, his collection of *Jacobite Relics*, and the many ballads and pastorals of his last two decades. Brief mention may be made of his droll mock-epic called 'Russiadde; a Fragment of an Ancient Epic Poem', in which the Shepherd laughs at his own cosmic myth-making. An earthy, Scottish hero named Russ falls in love with the moon, and is taken on her back 'through the yielding air, / Through bowels of the earth and sea'.[31] Even down in the underwater bower of Venus, Russ retains his stolid imperturbability:

> Russ was a fisher good and keen,
> At many a bout on Tweed had been,
> And still he kept an eager eye
> On every large one swagging bye.

Love, universal values, community, and profound simplicity are qualities of Hogg's shorter poems and songs. 'My Emma, my darling' was published in the 1831 *Songs, by the Ettrick Shepherd*, although it was written many years before. This delightful, direct piece tells of a youth who invites his sweatheart to

> fly to the glee of the city again,
> Where a day never wakes but some joy it renews,
> And a night never falls but that joy it pursues;
> Where the dance is so light, and the hall is so bright,
> And life whirls onward one round of delight.
> Would we feel that we love and have spirits refined,
> We must mix with the world, and enjoy humankind.

An unjustifiably neglected ballad is 'Cary O'Kean', Hogg's story (based on the Bounty mutiny of 1789) of an Irish sailor who falls in love with a Polynesian girl. O'Kean's speech as he sails away from his homeland is the first of several implied comparisons between the two islands of Ireland and Tahiti:

> Adieu! once lov'd country, thy name be forgot,
> For interest pervades thee, and feeling is not.
> I'll circle the earth, some sweet island to find,
> Where primitive innocence models the mind;
> Where nature blooms fair on the face of the free.[32]

After the dreadful events of this ballad, the poet concludes with a direct statement of James Hogg's belief in the possibility of reconciling natural and spiritual aspects of human life:

> But there is a feeling engrafted on mind,
> A shoot of eternity never defin'd,
> That upward still climbs to its origin high;
> Its roots are in nature, it blooms in the sky.

James Hogg was fifty years old in 1820, the year of his marriage. His appearance had not improved with age. A Glasgow student saw him in 1818 as a 'thick, sturdy, blowsy, looking fellow' who 'had the appearance of a porter to cudgel our worthy townsman'[33] — the townsman being John Douglas, editor of Glasgow's *Chronicle* newspaper. John Lockhart, one of the new *Blackwood's* writers, gives this portrait of Hogg:

> His face and hands are still as brown as if he lived entirely
> *sub dio*. His very hair has a coarse stringiness about it, . . .
> and hangs in playful whips and cords about his ears, in a
> style of the most perfect innocence imaginable. His mouth, .
> . . when he smiles, nearly cuts the totality of his face in twain
> . . . for his teeth have been allowed to grow where they
> listed, presenting more resemblance in arrangement, (and
> colour too,) to a body of crouching sharp-shooters.

Still, the great phrenologist Dr Spurzheim could detect 'marks of genius in the cranium of the pastoral poet', according to Lockhart, who pictures the popular craniologist eagerly examining a skeptical Hogg '— and some cranioscopical young ladies of Edinburgh are said still to practise in the same way upon the good-humoured owner of so many fine bumps'.[34]

Notes

1 Hogg, 'Memoir', p. 30
2 Gillies, *Memoirs*, II, 127.
3 *Pollock's New Guide Through Edinburgh* (Edinburgh, 1834), p. 138.
4 'Christopher North', in 'Noctes Ambrosianae', XXIX, *Blackwood's Magazine*, Nov. 1826, p. 770.
5 Gillies, *Memoirs*, II, 188, 128.
6 Hogg, 'Memoir', p. 32.
7 Anon. rev. in *Eclectic Review*, Feb. 1817, p. 175.
8 Anon. revs. in *British Critic*, Jan. 1817, p. 97; *British Lady's Magazine*, Oct. 1816, p. 253; *Scots Magazine*, June 1816, p. 449; and *Antijacobin Review*, June 1817, p. 335.
9 Rev. Thomas Thomson, 'Prefatory Notice' to Hogg's *Mador of the Moor*, in *The Works of the Ettrick Shepherd*, ed. Thomson, 2 vols. (1865; rev. London, Edinburgh, and Glasgow, 1874), II, 104.
10 Letter to Bernard Barton, 14 May 1813, NLS 3278, f. 64.
11 G. T., 'Lines on James Hogg, the Ettrick Shepherd', *British Lady's Magazine*, Dec. 1816, p. 407.
12 Smith, *James Hogg* (Boston, 1980), p. 133.
13 Gifford, rev. of Smith's *James Hogg*, *Scottish Literary Journal*, supplement no. 17 (Winter 1982), p. 87.
14 Anon., 'On the Genius of Hogg', *Literary Speculum*, 2 vols. (London, 1822), II, 441.
15 Letter to Murray, 26 Dec. 1814, printed in Samuel Smiles, *A Publisher and His Friends*, 3 vols. (London, 1891), I, 344.
16 Anon. revs. in *Scots Magazine*, Dec. 1814, p. 932; *North American Review*, June 1819, pp. 15, 23; *Salopian Magazine*, May 1815, p. 239; *Eclectic Review*, Mar. 1815, p. 280; and *Augustan Review*, May 1815, p. 30.
17 Hogg, 'Memoir', pp. 32, 33.
18 Hogg, 'Connel of Dee', in his *Winter Evening Tales*, 2 vols. (Edinburgh and London, 1820), II, 204-22.
19 Hogg, 'On Carmel's Brow', in his *Sacred Melodies* (London, 1815); rpt. in *The Poetical Works of James Hogg*, 4 vols. (Edinburgh and London, 1822), IV, 223-24.
20 Hogg, 'Superstition', appended to his *Pilgrims of the Sun* (Edinburgh and London, 1815), pp. 131-48.
21 Hogg, 'Memoir', p. 40.
22 Anon. revs. in *Lady's Magazine*, Feb. 1825, p. 97; *Literary Cynosure*, 22 Jan. 1825, p.14; *Westminster Review*, Apr. 1825, p. 531; *Philomathic Journal*, Apr. 1825, p. 161; *Edinburgh Observer*, 22 Dec. 1824, p. 4; *Literary Gazette*, 25 Dec. 1824, p. 817; *Ayr Correspondent*, 31 Dec. 1824, p. 29; and *Monthly Critical Gazette*, Mar. 1825, p. 343.
23 Hogg, 'Memoir', p. 69.
24 Byron, letter to Thomas Moore, 3 Aug. 1814, rpt. in *Byron's Letters and Journals*, ed. Marchand, 12 vols. (London, 1975-82), IV, 152.

25 Byron, letter to Hogg, 1 Mar. 1816, rpt. in *Byron's Letters and Journals*, V, 38.
26 Anon. rev. in *British Lady's Magazine*, May 1816, p. 385.
27 Hogg, letter to John Murray, 7 May 1815, rpt. in Strout, *Life and Letters of James Hogg*, p. 258.
28 Wilson, letter to Jane Wilson, printed in Mary Gordon, '*Christopher North*': *A Memoir of John Wilson* (Edinburgh, 1862), p. 186.
29 Gillies, *Memoirs*, II, 242, 243.
30 [Lockhart], *Peter's Letters to his Kinsfolk*, 3 vols. (Edinburgh, 1819), III, 140-41.
31 Hogg, 'The Russiadde', in his *Poetical Works* (1822), III, 295-359. Unfortunately the commonest edition of Hogg's verse (—Thomson's *Works of the Ettrick Shepherd*—)omits the second half of 'The Russiade'.
32 'Cary O'Kean, A Poem: By James Hogg', *Scots Magazine*, Dec. 1821, pp. 575-81.
33 Anon. rev., 'Hogg's *Three Perils of Woman*', *Emmet*, 18 Oct. 1823, p. 25.
34 [Lockhart], *Peter's Letters*, I, 139, and II, 341.

Chapter Five

ARE THE MUNROES
OF FOULIS YOUR COUSINS?

Yesterday forenoon, a gentleman from Glasgow, whose
name had been impertinently introduced into Blackwood's
Magazine, horsewhipped [Blackwood] opposite to his own
shop in Prince's Street. As this gentleman was stepping into
the Glasgow coach, at four o'clock, MR BLACKWOOD, armed
with a bludgeon, and apparently somewhat intoxicated, and
accompanied by a man having the appearance of a shop
porter, attempted a violent assault, but without injury, the
attack being repelled and retaliated by the free use of the
horsewhip.

Glasgow Chronicle, 12 May 1818.

THE 'gentleman' in this account was the *Chronicle*'s editor John
Douglas, angry at being lampooned as 'The Glasgow Gander' in
Blackwood's. The man who looked like a burly shop assistant was
James Hogg, acting as a body-guard for his intrepid new publisher William Blackwood. Blackwood would claim that after
Douglas had horsewhipped him he armed himself with 'a hazel
sapling' and summoned his 'much respected friend Mr. Hogg'.
The two men lay in seige for Douglas at the door of Mackay's
Hotel. When the Glasgow man finally ventured out to board the
four o'clock stage-coach, Blackwood 'proceeded to lay on him
with my stick', while 'Mr. Hogg stepped in and prevented all
further interference' from Douglas's companion. After giving 'at
least a dozen blows, as hard as I could lay them on', Blackwood
stood back on the pavement to shout, 'Now, you cowardly
scoundrel, you have got what will make you remember me, —
come down if you dare'. Douglas retreated into the coach and
returned to Glasgow.

James Hogg took offence at being compared to a shop porter,
and in a public advertisement he announced that he was 'a

frequent and welcome guest in companies where [Douglas] would not be admitted as a waiter'.[1] Highly affronted, the Gander came charging back to Edinburgh on a second errand of vengeance. He arrived on a hot, sunny Saturday, the twenty-third of May, this time with two friends, to challenge Hogg to a duel. The Shepherd invited the men into his room, then nimbly stepped out into the hallway himself and locked the door. After sending for the police, Hogg hurried down to Walter Scott's for legal advice. Scott's version of this affair makes fun of his friend's plebeian speech and very un-*Queen's Wake*-like behaviour: '[A]bout seven in the morning', Scott recalls,

> my servant announced while I was shaving in my dressing room that Mr Hogg wishd earnestly to speak to me. He was usherd in & . . . said scratching his head most vehemently 'Odd Scott here's twae fo'ks come frae Glasgow to provoke *mey* to fight a duel' — 'A duel' answerd I in great astonishment 'And what do you intend to do?' — 'Odd I lockd them up in my room & sent the lassie for twa o' the police & just gied the men ower to their charge. . . . '[2]

Scott might have liked to see a duel, but James Hogg stood firm on the side of discretion. He left the city for his Altrive farm that morning. Years later a poem by John Wilson commemorated this visit to Edinburgh by John Douglas, with his 'head held on high, and his rump drooping down':

> There was surely in Nature no sight so absurd
> As the aspect of this most preposterous bird:
> And surely no gabble was ever yet heard
>   Like that of the Gander of Glasgow,
>   The great gabbling Goose of the West.
>
> With pinions half-folded his course see him steer!
> Oh! if any one sight more grotesque could appear
> Than the Gander in front, 'twas the Gander in rear —
>   The rear of the Gander of Glasgow,
>   The rump of the Goose of the West![3]

Working for Blackwood involved Hogg in endless public controversies and private ambivalence. A satire called 'The

Chaldee Manuscript', written by Hogg and revised by Wilson and Lockhart, took an irreverent approach to the Bible and to Scotland's literary fraternity; it brought public outrage, several successful lawsuits against Blackwood, and of course a great increase in subscriptions. Hogg played no role in *Blackwood's* scurrilous treatment of Keats or Coleridge, nor did he share the magazine's snobbish, high-powered style of Toryism. He became a victim of *Blackwood's* slander through its notorious 'Noctes Ambrosianae' series, which until the end of his life portrayed the Shepherd as a kind of Caliban, boozing, brawling, and bragging. Hogg was dependent on Blackwood for the publication of his stories, yet he strongly resented the 'beastly usage' of him by Blackwood and his 'assassins':

> I know not what to do with that wretch — he will neither
> answer a letter nor regard me one way or other, and though
> I have a written promise . . . 'that my name should never be
> mentioned in his mag. without my own consent', yet you see
> how it is kept and how I am misrepresented to the world. I
> am neither a drunkard nor an idiot nor a monster of nature.
> Nor am I so Imbecile as never to have written a word of
> grammar in my life.[4]

Rival periodicals charged that this 'truly honest, worthy, open-hearted son of nature' was being unfairly represented by *Blackwood's* 'in a light as contemptible as it was ridiculous'. A London critic named John Scott, angered beyond words by *Blackwood's* persecution of Hogg and Keats, fought a duel in 1821 with Lockhart's friend John Christie, and was killed by him. In Edinburgh it was claimed that Hogg, 'so gifted, yet so open and artless', was the victim of a 'worthless gang', 'up to the ears in filth', who 'lost no opportunity of describing him as . . . stupid, blundering, and half an ideot in his intellects'.[5]

As well as turning towards prose after 1816, James Hogg increasingly tries to express his characteristic sense of irreducible mystery through more plausible plots, through explicable psychological states like dreams or hallucinations, or through the device of a perplexed, commonsensical narrator. There are some major exceptions, but in general Hogg begins to cultivate greater realism, to abandon his fantastic flying cats and horrified husbands, and also to emphasise mainly the lower half of the circle, the journey of descent.

The despairing journey into a fluid realm informs both imagery and structure in Hogg's first novel, *The Brownie of Bodsbeck*. A group of Scottish Covenanters, persecuted for their extreme political and religious beliefs, takes refuge in a damp, dark underground cavern to hide from Claverhouse and his Royalist troops. Nearly every page invokes the sense of an ever-present murky or watery underworld, as when the soldiers throw one of their dying victims 'into a deep hole in the morass, where he sunk in the mire and was seen no more',[6] or when an old woman, whose ears have been cut off, her cheek branded, her family executed, all because of her faith, calls out for sympathy,

> For man hasna pitied me, an' God hasna pitied me! I'm
> gaun down a floody water, down, down! an' I wad fain grip
> at something, if it war but a swoomin strae, as a last hope, or
> I sink a' thegither.[7]

The presence of this lower world allows Hogg to bridge the gap between the demands of realism and his existential sense of the uncertainty, chaos and horror at the centre of human life. Appropriately the brownies, ghosts, and demons who at first seem to represent this realm in *The Brownie of Bodsbeck* turn out to be Covenanters, persecuted human beings. In other words, the mysterious has primarily a *human* and *social* significance, on this earth. All of Hogg's major figures must confront this chaos, and their response to it defines their moral condition. The honest characters endure the descent with some equanimity and avoid judging others by appearances, while immature characters try to escape from mystery, either by assuming the worst (like the superstitious peasants who assume that the heroine, Katherine, is in league with the devil), or by rigidly maintaining narrow and overly-rational religious doctrines (like the Covenanters), or by demanding explicit statements of belief (like the inquisitor Claverhouse, whose mission is to find and exterminate the Covenanters). The fundamental lesson of charity, fellowship, and the acceptance of human nature is voiced by Katherine's father, when at the end he learns that his daughter, like himself, has secretly been helping the fugitives: 'Deil care what side they war

G

on, Kate!' he cries with relief; 'ye hae taen the side o' human nature; the suffering and the humble side, an' the side o' feeling, my woman'.[8] As in, say, 'Evil Speaking', the only mature response, the only convincing escape from chaos, is through the simple acceptance of the oneness of humanity. Their honest, courageous descent into confusion allows Katherine, her father, and James Hogg to accept mystery as a condition of life, to sympathise with people of different beliefs, and to see the human face underneath pretensions of intellect or dogma. Static characters like the Covenanters, on the one hand, or Claverhouse, on the other, never seem to perceive the universal meaning behind uncertainty, and never therefore discover their own affinity with their enemies.

Not surprisingly the London critics found 'vulgarity and nonsense' and 'ludicrous exaggeration' in *The Brownie*. The main obstacle to appreciation seems to have been Hogg's unflattering portrait of the Tory Claverhouse, which to many readers came close to being an attack on the aristocracy. One critic found *The Brownie of Bodsbeck* 'little more than a clumsy iteration of some of the events of [Scott's] *Old Mortality*', adding, 'What can be more disgusting than the Claverhouse of Hogg, after the highly finished portrait of the great Unknown?' But *The Scotsman*, a liberal Edinburgh paper, reacted more favourably: 'Mr Hogg displays . . . all the minuteness and fidelity of the Dutch masters'. *The Brownie*, said this critic, is 'adapted to intellects of all dimensions: the most obtuse will find matter for wonderment', while 'the most profound' will find food 'for reflection', and 'all will be amused'.[9]

A more experimental use of water-imagery occurs in Hogg's long story 'The Wool-Gatherer'. This tale is a re-write of *The Spy*'s 'Country Laird'. Lindsey, a young, intellectual, mother-dominated laird, has set aside his books and journals to learn the art of fishing, but without much success: 'He pulled out the line, and threw it in again so fast, that he appeared more like one threshing corn'.[10] Returning to the stream the next day, he meets a young woman standing in a pool and 'gathering the small flakes of wool . . . that had fallen from the sheep in washing'. The Wool-Gatherer, Jane, is destitute and unmarried, with a child of two. Like Wordsworth's Leech-Gatherer she represents common humanity living in a state of nature and apparently without any cultural or social advantages. Lindsey returns each day to the clear, deep pool, until Jane is suddenly evicted from the estate by his mother.

Jane is then homeless until she meets up with a shepherd named Barnaby, who takes her and her child to his parents' cottage, which happens to stand 'at the confluence of two rough but clear mountain streams, that ran one on each side of the house'. On their long walk the shepherd recounts many of his dreams and experiences of *deja vu*: 'dreams, visions, and apparitions, were Barnaby's region of existence'. He tells her the story of a housemaid, seduced by a laird, who

> was never seen again, nor heard of mair in this world! But there war some banes found about the Alemore Loch that the doctors said had belanged to a woman. There was some yellow hair, too, on the scull, that was unco like Molly's, but nae body could say.

With Jane at his parents', Barnaby returns to the stream where he meets Lindsey. Each man wants to learn what the other knows about Jane, without betraying what he himself knows. Barnaby, impatient at watching the laird trying to fish, then offers to teach him to 'gump'. The scene that follows might almost have been written by D. H. Lawrence:

> Down this narrow vale the Tod Burn ran with a thousand beautiful serpentine windings, and at every one of these turns there were one or two clear deep pools, overhung by little green banks. Into the first of these pools Barnaby got with his staff, plunging and poaching to make all the fish take into close cover; then he threw off his ragged coat, tucked up the sleeves of his shirt to the shoulders, tying them together behind, and into the pool he got again, knees and elbows, putting his arms in below the green banks, into the closest and most secret recesses of the trouts. There was no eluding him; he threw them out one after another, sometimes hitting the astonished laird on the face, or any other part of the body without ceremony, for his head being down sometimes close with the water, and sometimes below it, he did not see where he flung them. . . .
>   . . .In short, it was not long till the laird was to be seen

wading in the pools, and *gumping* as busily as the other; and, finally, he was sometimes so intent on his prey, that the water was running over his back, so that when he raised himself up it poured in torrents from his fine Holland shirt and stained cambrick ruffles.

Lindsey, rich, remote, and intellectual, shakes off his reserve, climbs into the water, and implicitly affirms the primacy of physical existence and his affinity with his opposite Barnaby.

Hogg's fascination with water in 'The Wool-Gatherer' conveys his sense of a non-rational underworld embracing the womb, mystery, dreams, sexuality, suffering, and death. Yet for all its integrity of images and theme, the story ends disappointingly with a typical romance wind-up complete with vindicated heroine, chastened villain (Lindsey's mother), and a happy ending for all. It turns out that the child was the son of Jane's sister, who had died in giving birth. Uncertain whether her sister had been married or not, Jane had simply allowed people to assume that the child was her own. In the last paragraph Lindsey marries Jane and hires Barnaby to manage their estate. Hogg is clearly trying to flatter his affluent readers with a 'pure' heroine and a cosy resolution that assuages any moral or social anxieties which the earlier part of the story might have aroused. 'The Wool Gatherer', 'one of the prettiest romaunts of common life . . . that we ever read',[11] as *The Scotsman* put it, was of course loudly applauded by the more respectable critics of 1818.

Most of Hogg's prose stories depict only the journey of descent, but 'The Wool-Gatherer' is one exception, as it briefly glimpses his old poetic idea of a ring formed by the two constrasting pathways. The fleeting reference to an ascending path occurs when Barnaby sees the smoke coming out of his parents' chimney: 'The rising sun kissed [the smoke] with his beams, which gave it a light woolly appearance, something like floating down; it was so like a vision that Barnaby durst scarcely look at it'. In this sentence the allusions to kissing, to a vision, and to 'floating', 'woolly' smoke, pointedly recall the earlier scene when Lindsey met Jane as she stood in a pool gathering wool. As in his *Midsummer Night Dreams*, Hogg is again using the sky as a mirror of what happens on earth. This implies that physical values are ultimately the mirror of spiritual values. The voyage downward into chaos and the physical, and the voyage upward into spirituality, have ultimately the same meaning, since each one leads to a lessening of pride and a discovery of social vision and community values. Whichever path or parabola they choose, the honest characters eventually learn the same basic lessons and end up at the same destination.

Too many readers find only a quaint credulity in Hogg's use of the supernatural. In fact his ghosts, brownies, visions and dreams always carry a symbolic and thematic significance, whatever their real status in the real world. Hogg's brownies and kelpies are a device to invoke the inexplicable, to keep alive different possibilities, and to save readers from the single vision that demands either literal-minded belief or disbelief. A reader who wants to dissolve these mysteries, to *know*, is actually like Claverhouse or the Covenanters, or like Lindsey's mother, or the foolish servant in Hogg's *The Long Pack*, who, confronted with a mysterious parcel, simply fires a rifle into it. The brownies of Bodsbeck quite significantly turn out to be human beings, while in 'The Wool-Gatherer' Barnaby's visions provide a kind of commentary on the descent into chaos by Lindsey and Jane. For example, Barnaby asks Jane, '[H]ave ye never, when you saw a thing for the first time, had a distinct recollection of having seen it sometime afore?' This question is not so much Barnaby's reference to *deja vu*, as Hogg's challenge to the reader to notice the constant recurrence of water-images in both the supernatural tales of Barnaby, and the realistic adventures of Lindsey and Jane herself. Supernatural possibilities, like physical realities, should be seen in Hogg's work mainly in relation to the human journey that gives them meaning. In symbolic terms, we should try to understand the precise parallel between Barnaby's 'vision' of wool-like smoke rising in the sky 'like floating down', and Jane's attempt to earn a living by collecting wool from pools of water.

Many of the tales of Hogg's last two decades will simply present mysteries and leave the reader to work out symbolic, thematic meaning in the absence of any factual assurances. A clergyman's dying speech in one of Hogg's dramas is a good example of his provoking readers to confront uncertainty: 'I taught the way through Christ',[12] the old man says, 'Because no other surely led to peace',

But when I 'thought me of the human millions
Swept off by famine, pestilence, and sword,
From Adam down to this — the serf, the savage,
The infidel, the sage — men of all casts,
Tenets, beliefs, strewed o'er the world's wide face,
From age to age, like carrion — why, I doubted;
Though zealous to believe, I doubted sore.

This dying, doubt-riddled 'champion' has a mature vision shaped
by uncertainty, by accepting challenge and chaos, and by humane
love;

I've thought, and thought, and preached, and prayed,
And doubted: thought, and preached, and prayed, again,
And all that I have reached is a resolve
To take my chance with others — and I'll do it!

One of James Hogg's most popular ventures, particularly in
America, where it went through countless editions after his death,
was the *Winter Evening Tales*. Many of these tales are extended
revisions of sketches from *The Spy*. Even the altered titles
indicate a development away from didacticism towards a cultivation of mystery: 'Dangerous Consequences of the Love of Fame'
now becomes simply 'Adam Bell', while 'Evil Speaking Ridiculed
by an Allegorical Dream' resurfaces as 'Singular Dream', and
'Misery of an Old Batchelor' turns into the 'Love Adventures of
Mr George Cochrane'.

Another *Spy* story, 'The Danger of Changing Occupations',
was greatly expanded to become 'The Renowned Adventures of
Basil Lee'. In North America the roguish hero falls in love with
Clifford, a woman from Inverness. Basil's love for Clifford is
undiminished by the news that she had been a street-walker in
Scotland. Their long affair ends amicably when Clifford marries a
wealthy American. Basil sails for home, is shipwrecked off the Isle
of Lewis, and wanders southward through the Highlands, meeting with several supernatural events that involve ghosts or the
second sight. Happening to meet Clifford's father, now a beggar
in Inverness, Basil gives him some money. In Edinburgh he
grows old, falls into debt, and prepares to wed a horrible rich
woman with whiskers. Luckily Clifford suddenly appears in the
city, explains that her husband has died, and she and Basil forgive

each other's failings and marry happily. 'Basil Lee' is highly amoral by orthodox standards, but it finds a deeper morality by tracing Hogg's personal myth of descent through the stages of individualism, suffering, the physical, extreme mystery, and finally an affirmation of community and love.

This distinctive journey informs all of Hogg's prose fictions, although the pattern is not always as obvious as it is in *The Brownie of Bodsbeck*, 'The Wool-Gatherer', or 'Basil Lee'. His wonderfully ironic 'Love Adventures of Mr George Cochrane' shows what happens when a protagonist fails to learn the essential lesson of fellowship. George's first two lovers (following the 1810 version) are a servant and a woman of high social standing; these are now joined by a third lover, Catholic, a fourth, extreme Presbyterian, and a fifth, who is devout but moderate. George's five affairs are a vehicle for Hogg's survey of Scottish society, with suggestive allusions and parallels to emphasise the underlying social or religious divisons. With his third mistress, the Catholic Mary, George Cochrane comes to grief when he misunderstands her use of the saints' calendar; arriving twenty-four hours late for their secret tryst (which had been set for 'the eve of Locherbie fair') the hero tries to save himself by arguing:

'My dear Mary', said I, 'surely you will not pretend to assert that the evening of a fair day is not the fair eve!' 'Are you so childishly ignorant', returned she, 'as not to know that the eve of a festival, holiday, or any particular day whatever, always precedes the day nominally?' I denied the position positively, in all its parts and bearings. She reddened; and added, that she could not help pitying a gentleman who knew so little of the world, and the terms in use among his countrymen — terms with which the meanest hind in the dale was perfectly well acquainted. 'Pray, consider', added she, 'do you not know that the night before a wedding, the night on which we throw the stocking, is always denominated the wedding eve? All-Hallow eve, the night on which we burn the nuts, pull the kail stocks, and use all our cantrips, is the evening before Hallow-day. St Valentine's eve, and Fasten's eve, are the same. Why then will you set up your own recent system against the sense and understanding of a whole country?'

95

'Never tell me of your old Popish saws and customs; the whole of your position is founded in absurdity, my love', said I. 'This, you know, is the evening of the fair day — the fair is doubtless going on as merrily as ever; this then must either be the fair eve, or else the fair has two eves . . . '.

'I could go further back, and to higher authority, than old Popish saws, as you call them, for the establishment of my position, if I chose', said she; 'I could take the account of the first formation of the day and the night, where you will find it recorded, that 'the *evening* and the morning were the first day;' but as it would be a pity to mortify one by a confutation who is so wise in his own conceit, I therefore give up the argument. You are certainly in the right; and may you always profit in the same way as you have done now, by sticking to your own opinion'.

This was a severe one; and in the temper and disposition that I was in, not to be brooked. 'Nothing can be more plain', said I, 'than that the evening of a day is the evening of that day'.

'Nothing can', said she.

'And, moreover', said I, 'has not the matter been argued thoroughly by our christian divines?'

'It has', said she.

'And have not they all now agreed, from St Chrysostom down to Ebenezer Erskine, that the Sabbath-day begins in the morning?'

'They have', said she.

'And if the Sabbath begins in the morning, so must also Monday; and so must every day, whether fair day or festival'.

'There is no doubt of it at all', said she. . . . [13]

Passages like this are a high-spirited burlesque of the religious disputes that have plagued Scotland through the centuries. Hogg's own perspective is approximately equidistant from the two stubborn antagonists, Catholic and Protestant. His delicate comic balance conveys the ideal of moderation and love, together with the reality of schism.

Religious differences bring verbal disputes when George courts Mary, but when he turns to the Cameronian (or extreme Presbyterian) Jessy, he must submit to a more physical and literal form of wrangling. A rival tells him, 'If ever tou gangs to court the lassie, as I hae deune mony a time, tou maun first thraw a' the wooers that are there at a worstle, or the deil a word tou gets o' her'. The beautiful but mischievous and teasing Jessy insists that prospective lovers compete for her favours in wrestling matches, 'just as ane could warstle himsel into heaven', as her grumbling mother puts it.

A four-line quotation from Byron's *Don Juan* near the end of the 'Love Adventures' confirms its debunking, satirical spirit. Yet ultimately Hogg's vision is quite different from Byron's, since rather than reducing spiritual values to physical ones the Shepherd tries to reconcile the two perspectives, drawing a full circuit of human experience that, ideally, would encompass both spiritual wisdom and physical realities. In his 'Love Adventures' the Shepherd plays on the dichotomy of spiritual and physical love through frequent expressions like 'this angel of a woman' or 'saintly charmer'. At times these double meanings can be quite daring; when Jessy's mother complains that, 'a cast o' grace thou'lt never get', Jessy replies, 'Indeed, but I will, mwother: an thou'lt gae to thee bed, [George Cochrane] will gi'e me ane'.

All of George's affairs end in confusion and disaster. They are like 'meteors in the paths of folly, gilding the prospects of youth for a season with rays of the warmest and most brilliant hues', but leaving 'the headlong follower' to 'pursue his devious course in darkness and uncertainty'. His most disastrous relationship is the one with Jessy, which gives him a fractured skull, a coma, and twelve months of 'swimming in my head'. The fifth and last lover is more understanding, and has the extra advantage of being well-to-do. This 'young lady of forty-five' becomes disillusioned with the hero, however, when he comes into conflict with 'the minister and kirk-session of the parish . . . because, forsooth, I would not submit to do penance publicly in the church, a foolish and injurious old popish rite, which I despised'. Barred from taking the sacraments, George must 'sit cocking up in the corner of the front gallery all alone' under the astonished gaze of his new sweetheart; 'I was all by myself, there not being one of the same station near me; and to make the matter worse, the precentor, as he bawled out the following line, looked full at me, — "Beside thee there is none!"'' George Cochrane is an outcast from community, an isolated individual imprisoned in his pride: 'I would not stand up', he insists, 'in my native parish church before a whole congregation, to every one of whom I was personally known, not only to be rebuked, but to hear the most gross and indelicate terms mouthed as applying to my character, and that with an assured gravity of deportment, which makes the scene any thing but impressive, save on the organs of risibility'. Locked in pride, George is condemned to frustrated bachelorhood and alienation from his society. There can be no marriage, no birth, no symbolic, unifying Advent, at the end of these adventures.

In some ways George Cochrane can be seen as a precursor to Robert Wringhim in the *Confessions*. He endures the descent into the purely physical, and into confusion, and like Wringhim he never perceives the one very simple essential truth that might lead to harmony and fulfilment. George never sees that all people are the same, united by their involvement in physical processes and their nearness to chaos. He never sees that his real enemy is his own individualism, pride, or ego. But if George remains fixed at the merely physical, some of the women he pursues foreshadow a different side of Robert Wringhim in remaining fixated at an equally inadequate stage of *spiritual* development. Both Mary and the fifth woman are imprisoned by their own elitist illusions of belonging to the 'correct' faith or having 'correct' or superior morals.

Critics shuddered at the 'great many vulgarisms' of the *Winter Evening Tales*, yet they were not completely blind to other aspects of its realism. John Scott's *London Magazine* found 'downright vulgarity and nonsense' offset by 'genius', an 'exquisite delicacy of thought, and light grace of manner'. To one reader the tales seemed 'thrown together in a rather crude and undigested shape', while to *Blackwood's* they were 'written . . . with the utmost simplicity — they breathe the very spirit of the man that tells them'. This critic however went on to warn the author against language 'which would make the faces of young ladies in ballrooms . . . blush blue as their stockings': 'Mr Hogg', it was said, 'is too fond of calling some things by their plain names, which would be better expressed by circumlocution'. An ingenious critic in *The Scotsman* found the *Tales* 'unquestionably the work of a man of genius', and rated Hogg above Walter Scott, but strongly advised the author to marry, in order that 'before the book again see the public, he read the whole over to his wife, and strike out every paragraph which . . . offends her delicacy'.[14]

As it happened James Hogg anticipated this advice by marrying, the day before, his friend Margaret Phillips. Margaret was a practical woman, a farmer's daughter, almost twenty years younger than James. Their relationship seems to have been genuinely loving, although there is a trace of irony when James writes, 'Indeed so uniformly smooth and happy has my married life been, that on a retrospect I cannot distinguish one part from another, save by some remarkably good days of fishing, shooting, and curling on the ice'.[15] 'I have a most amiable, virtuous and kind hearted young lady for my spouse', James would explain to a London poet in 1828; 'One son and three daughters all blooming, healthy and happy creatures and as for me I have hitherto been uniformly happy in all circumstances and thankful and truly grateful for my lot'.[16]

Their first child arrived in March 1821. Wanting a larger house and feeling confident they could succeed in farming on a larger scale, the Hoggs took a nine-year lease on the neighbouring farm, Mount Benger. 'I have got 300 ewes and 223 lambs on the farm, a compleat set of labouring utensils, two middling horses, and about half a stock of cattle', wrote James in June 1821; 'I have sown 22 acres of turnips and four of potatoes, and am going to do everything I can do'.[17] The lease on Mount Benger was a disaster, leaving James and Margaret with a high, fixed rent in a decade of continuing depression, falling prices, and London governments which tended to side either with rich land-owners or with the new urban populace. In desperation James turned to his writing, ploughing out dozens of inoffensive stories and saleable poems and turfing the profits back into the farm. Although as an author the Shepherd earned close to a thousand pounds in the first two years of their marriage, Mount Benger left Margaret and him literally 'without a sixpence in the world'.[18] Still, poor as they were, James could make pens out of goose quills and even his own ink concocted from 'a little gunpowder & soot mixt wi' water'.[19]

Every one of Hogg's longer works tries to interpret the past and prophesy for the future. His *Three Perils of Man; or, War, Women, and Witchcraft* assesses the past through a tale of fourteenth-century wars of chivalry between the English and Scots, as well as through a structure derived from medieval romance. The first stage of the journey now becomes the proud rivalry of two young coquettes, Princess Margaret of Scotland and Lady Jane Howard of England. Lord Musgrave and his English soldiers have invaded Scotland and captured Roxburgh Castle, which they promise to keep as a pledge of Musgrave's love for Lady Howard; the Scots are attempting to recapture the castle, as a pledge of *their* leader's, Lord Douglas's, love for Princess Margaret. Meanwhile Sir Ringan Redhough, uncertain whether to side with the Scots or English, sends his retainer Charlie Scott and several others on a journey to the tower of Michael Scott. The wizard Michael Scott will apparently be able to predict which army is going to win, and this information will be quite handy to Sir Ringan in deciding whose side to take.

It is this long journey to the wizard's tower, this comic descent into the demonic, which occupies the central chapters of *The Three Perils of Man*. At different times on their journey the seven pilgrims find themselves each divided into two separate persons, see a man blown apart by dynamite, encounter a monster, 'half-man and half-beast',[20] and are momentarily turned into animals themselves. As well as being the traditional stuff of medieval romance, these episodes are exactly placed to express Hogg's themes of the fragility of the human self, the illusoriness of normal existence, and the animal side of human nature. What in former works had been an underworld of ambivalence, chaos, or materialism, now becomes the 'inverted medium'[21] of black magic, a nightmare realm of demonic illusion, inversion, and transformation. As one character says, everything is 'turned upside-down':

> The trees hae turned their wrang ends upmost — the waters hae drowned the towns, and the hills hae been rent asunder and riddled up like heaps o' chaff. 'Tis thought that there has been a seige o' hell, and that the citadel has been won, for the deils are a' broken loose and rinning jabbering through the land.[22]

A lazy or naive reader will be spellbound by these events, like that hapless heroine 'poor Alice', in a satirical novel published in London in 1824; poor Alice, after reading Hogg's '*delightful* border romance of "War, Women, and Witchcraft"', falls in love with 'her dear *Etrick Shepherd*',[23] then announces her intention of walking barefoot to Scotland to meet the author, and finally goes off the deep end when she and her sister start traipsing around London dressed as the two heroines of *The Three Perils of Man*. A good reader, however, will notice the allegory of Hogg's novels, and foresee the necessary result of the descent, which of course ends with the pilgrims being imprisoned within Michael Scott's tower. By a master-stroke of plotting Hogg arranges for the wizard himself to be trapped along with his victims. The captive, frightened, starving pilgrims must now confront their physical natures.

To pass the time and allay their fears, the prisoners hold a story-telling contest. They agree that whoever tells the poorest story will be eaten by the others. The first, 'The Friar's Tale', tells of the seduction and death of a young girl and the enslavement of her people. The second yarn is about a youth so hungry for rich meat that he steals bacon, steals a lamb, and finally murders a man to keep himself well fed. Next, a story by Charlie Scott describes past border atrocities between English and Scots, each side devoted to torturing, killing, and robbing the other. A fourth story tells of a hungry servant who secretly murders his master's ox, sees another man convicted for the offence, and lives a life of deceit, theft, and imprisonment.

After the fourth tale the contest is interrupted by the arrival of friendly knights who promise to rescue the pilgrims and then ride away to get help. The last narrative then describes a victory over materialism by three Scottish maidens who resist their Viking captors. The maidens are (apparently) martyred and receive eternal life. Since this fifth story is told when the travellers are expecting to be rescued, it takes the optimistic form of a miniature romance, ending with a symbolic triumph over the physical.

Each of the five chronicles follows a descending path into a realm of physical compulsion represented by lust, gluttony, vengeance, torture, captivity, slavery, suffering, or death. Except in the final tale, there appears to be no escape from this lower world, with every act of betrayal, vengeance, exploitation or greed only giving rise to further atrocities. The stories confirm and clarify the over-all shape of *The Three Perils of Man*; they strip away pretensions to show the human condition at its lowest and most physical. However, through listening to each others' tales,

101

the pilgrims also learn that they are related in various ways: for example, the villain of the second piece is none other than Tam Craig himself, one of the story-tellers, while the child rescued in Charlie Scott's anecdote turns out to be the poet, another member of the group. In this rudimentary way the five narratives conform to Hogg's practice of using fictions to show the way to freedom through an implied recognition of relationship, human unity, and fellowship.

With all its surface excitement of heroic action, comedy, and the supernatural, *The Three Perils of Man* is chiefly remarkable for an intelligent structure combining allegorical romance with Hogg's characteristic myth of descent. Of the seven travellers, the five least materialistic are finally set free from the tower, although this can only happen when their rescuers enlist the help of a certain devilish character, 'no other than the prince of the power of the air, the great controller of the mighty elements'.[24] The difficult, even dangerous implication of this passage can be approached by way of one critic's comment on Spenser's *Faerie Queene*: 'our world is dualistic for all practical purposes, dualistic in all but the very last resort: but from the final heresy [the author] abstains, drawing back from the verge of dualism to remind us by delicate allegories that though the conflict seems ultimate yet one of the opposites really contains, and is not contained by, the other'.[25]

As soon as they are free, the wizard at last agrees to show them 'the manner, and very mode, by which your captain must only hope to succeed in his great enterprise'.[26] Abruptly he casts a spell on Charlie and the others, turning them into cattle, and announcing, 'I have now given you your own proper shapes, and showed you in frames suited to your natures'.[27] This final, puzzling horror ends when the friar restores the pilgrims to their ordinary human forms.

In the last chapters Hogg clarifies the meaning of these episodes and again displays his wonderful talent for expressing wisdom through careful nuances of structure and irony. Like a good reader, Charlie Scott tries to find universal meaning in his experience of descent. Back in the real world he reflects on Michael Scott's enigmatic last words, until suddenly he has the illuminating idea of dressing himself in the skins of cattle. That is, he will use art (or disguise) to imitate what the wizard had achieved through black magic. This allows him, along with Sir Ringan, to be driven into Roxburgh Castle in the midst of a herd of oxen. Once inside the walls, the two warriors throw off their disguises, lock the English soldiers outside the gates, and recapture Roxburgh for Scotland. The act of dressing in ox hides is the turning-point in the romance, the action that leads from despair to triumph and harmony: allegorically, it implies that mankind may reascend to its rightful place in an improved world only after fully accepting its universal, common bond in the physical or animal side of its nature.

But the need to acccept nature is only one half of the meaning of Charlie's action. The other side, equally important, is the role of art in transforming existence through the discovery or creation of allegories, symbols, or myths. Charlie Scott sees man's affinity with the animals (—the cattle—), yet he rises above the merely physical by finding a creative way of using that knowledge to alleviate present human conditions. His imagination is what turns the journey of descent into a movement towards freedom; a humiliating and demonic transformation of people into cattle, in Michael Scott's tower, now becomes, through the magic of art, a means of expressing profound truth, restoring social unity, and freeing human potential. Charlie Scott is Hogg's type of artist-hero, a person who fully confronts human frailty, travels down to the lowest point of despair, and in the end finds the road to recovery.

A few more ironic surprises near the end of *The Three Perils of Man* indicate that James Hogg also sees clearly the *limitations* of allegorical romance. Throughout the work he has undermined the traditions of chivalry, showing us the cruelty of warfare and the vanity of courtly love. And although the freeing of Roxburgh follows a typical romance ending, it also invites real sympathy for the trapped foreign soldiers, 'piled in a heap higher than a man's height, which was moving with agonized life from top to bottom, and from the one end to the other; for the men having all fallen by sword wounds, few of them were quite dead'.[28] Patriotism and militarism, then, are only partial, temporary solutions. The unity of Scotland is a worthwhile goal, but the ultimate goal, as almost all of Hogg's fictions imply, is the unity of the human race. In a final twist of irony, a kind of concluding unpatriotic postscript, the Shepherd arranges a marriage between Charlie, a Scotsman of relatively low birth, and Lady Jane of England.

The Three Perils of Man attracted little attention in its day, which was fortunate, since the few reviews which appeared were even more literal-minded than usual. It was 'clumsy and childish', said one critic; 'pimpled with coarseness, indelicacy, and profaneness', said another, adding an admonition to the author against a fourth peril of man, '— the peril of publishing nonsense'. Reviewers seldom bothered to look for the *ideas* that always invigorated Hogg's best work. The *Monthly Magazine* suggested that 'Though the first volume is in parts finely and powerfully written, the story begins to droop and fall away sadly'. Another critic pronounced a summary verdict:

> Of the Perils of Man, an ill written, disgusting, and absurd volume, the public has formed an opinion, and we trust the author will not again venture on so flagrant a trespass against common sense and decency. That any printer should be foolish enough to waste paper and labour on such trash, is truly surprising.[29]

What is truly surprising is that James Hogg continued to improve steadily as a first-rate artist despite the inane standards of popular fiction and the complacent objections of most critics. Always experimenting, always finding new ways of seeing, Hogg developed a kind of personal dialectic, a habit of progressing through opposite perspectives, of turning from objective to subjective, from Romantic to ironic, from tragic to comic, from present to past to future. His emphasis in *The Three Perils of Man* is allegorical, objective, and public, while in his next main work, a complementary piece called *The Three Perils of Woman*, the predominant tone is emotional, subjective, and private.

The Three Perils of Woman contains three separate but related stories. In the first, the two heroines Gatty and Cherry are both in love with a Highlander named Diarmid McIon. Gatty, though 'a prey to the most romantic and uncontrollable love', vows to honour 'the sacred bounds of virgin decorum'. Her cousin Cherry, on the contrary, has evidently been listening to Jane Austen's Marianne Dashwood, whom she echoes in exclaiming, 'I will always think as I feel, and express what I think . . . and if I should love Mr McIon ever so well, and die for him too, what has any body to say?'

A technique often found in nineteenth-century women's novels is the presentation of contrasting temperaments in two sisters or two female cousins. Scott's *Heart of Midlothian*, Susan Ferrier's *Marriage*, and Austen's *Sense and Sensibility* all conform to this model of balancing a 'good' heroine against a 'bad' or misguided heroine. The story of Gatty and Cherry will adapt this fictional convention, bending it to Hogg's idea of two paths uniting to form a ring. Gatty, with her proper attitudes, will try the ascending path of spirituality, while cousin Cherry, impetuous and improper, chooses the lower path that leads down to the physical. But in this work James Hogg begins to dismantle his long-held concept of the two journeys, to show for the first time that the pathways are intertwined and inseparable.

The two paths are first introduced through a dream of Cherry's. Falling asleep in Gatty's arms, she dreams that her cousin has

gone to a lovely place far above me, and I could not reach you, and neither would you return to me. And then I thought I saw hangings of gold and velvet, and a thousand chandeliers, all burning brighter than the sun; and I saw you dressed in gold, and diamonds, and bracelets of rubies; and you had a garland of flowers on your head. And then I wept and called long, but you would not answer me, for I was grieved at being left behind. And I saw a winding-path through flowery shrubs, and ran alongst it, asking every one whom I saw, if that was the way; and they all said, 'Yes.' . . . and so I ran on, till at length I saw you far above me, farther than ever. And then you called out, 'Dear cousin Cherry, you shall never get here by that path. Do you not see that tremendous precipice before you?' — 'Yes I do', said I; 'but that is a delightful flowery bank, and the path is sweet to the senses! O suffer me to go by that road!' — 'Nay, but when you come to that steep, the path is of glass', said you; 'and you will slide and fall down into an immeasurable void, and you will be lost, and never see this abode of beauty. Remember I have told you, for the name of that rock is LOVE'.

You then went away from my sight, and as soon as I saw you were gone, I took my own way, and followed the flowery path; and when I came to the rock, the walks were all of

105

glass, and I missed my footing and hung by some slender shrubs, calling out for help. At length young [McIon] . . . came to my assistance; but, instead of relieving me, he snapped my feeble support, and down I fell among rocks, and precipices, and utter darkness; and I shrieked aloud, and behold I was lying puling in your bosom, and you were speaking to me, and I cannot tell whether I was asleep or not.

The sentimentality, the fascination with ornaments, draperies, and rich furnishings, the use of dreams as omens, and the strong dose of youthful love and impending danger, are the typical stock of nineteenth-century polite romance, just as chivalry and magic (in *The Three Perils of Man*) were the stock-in-trade of medieval romance. If this dream episode is read in the context of Hogg's symbolism of the two journeys, however, we can begin to appreciate ironic possibilities which must have eluded most of his contemporary female audience. As in the *Midsummer Night Dreams*, the higher path, although more respectable, righteous, and prosperous, will have in the end the same human meaning and destination as the lower path; Gatty's apparent superiority, therefore, is an illusion, a temporary stage in a process which will soon bring her down to the same level as Cherry. And although Gatty imagines she is on the upward path, her journey will actually be a descent, a parallel to Cherry's.

Everything that happens between the two cousins helps to blur distinctions between conventional notions of good and evil. Gatty, playing hard to get, is rude to McIon, who then proposes to Cherry instead. McIon then learns that he is heir to a Highland estate. Suddenly Gatty renews her interest, and Cherry, seeing that McIon still loves Gatty, releases him from his promise of marriage. At the wedding, Cherry, acting as the bridesmaid, falls into a trance, with embarrassing results:

McIon's hand was already extended: the bride gave her maiden a quick tap on the arm to remind her of her duty; Cherry started as from a dream, but, instead of pulling off her cousin's gloves, she stretched out her hand to put it into the bridegroom's. That hand did not open to receive hers. Poor little Cherry's hand was turned aside; and the bride, ashamed of the delay on her part, was obliged to pull off her own glove with her left hand, and finally gave her hand to her lover, and with it herself for ever. — Cherry clasped her hands together, cowered down, and looked in their faces; then, again assuming her upright position, her eyes rolled about from one face to another so rapidly as to shew that her mind was bewildered.

After the wedding Cherry lives with Gatty and her husband, and we soon hear that McIon 'devotes those attentions to the maid that should be paid to the married wife'. Cherry falls ill with a mysterious disease, predicts her own death, and dies accordingly. (It seems likely that Hogg expected his readers to assume that this unnameable illness is in fact a venereal infection.) At the funeral Gatty cries, 'But I have murdered her!' and wishes 'that we were both laid in one grave on the same day'. Gatty too becomes ill, and McIon predicts that she is following her cousin to the grave, but instead of dying Gatty falls into a coma, a state of 'mere idiotism'. These events underscore the affinity between the 'good' cousin and the 'bad' cousin, with both women descending into the unconscious through their dreams, visions, fainting-fits, trances, terminal illness, or coma. By enduring this nightmarish realm, the heroines also confront the relativity of the self, of social conventions, and of morality.

Gatty awakens from her long coma, learns that she has given birth to a son, and afterwards tries to assert the hard-earned lesson of human unity, so that to 'all her friends' she becomes 'the joy, the life, and the bond of unity'. Symbolically she has lost the self and found community. Through her descent into the unconscious Gatty learns to renounce rivalry, to see the deep, primitive oneness of mankind, and, on returning to the everyday world, to affirm that underlying kinship on a conscious, social level through acts of love and charity.

In many ways the first tale of *The Three Perils of Woman* is a typical woman's romance for its time, with its sense of horror lurking at the edges of middle-class life and its blatantly symbolic conclusion. Only in retrospect, after reading the second story, a comedy, and the third, a tragedy, are we likely to sense the author's subversive intention. Each of the three parts is a fragmented re-working of Euripides' play *Ion*; the three pieces are also united through similar imagery and structure, with three descending journeys, three rivalries, three duels or intended duels, three sets of 'cousins', and three births at the end. As a whole *The Three Perils of Woman* is a daring experiment in the use of fictional genres, a work which begins by flattering its original audience with a happy middle-class romance, but then traces a similar general contour through the less idealising genres of comedy and tragedy. It provokes readers to notice connections underlying different categories of literature and different levels of life in a class society.

The middle part of *The Three Perils of Woman* is the narrative of Richard Rickleton. Richard, another cousin of Gatty and Cherry, is a ludicrous man who discovers that his bride Cathrine is 'very much addicted to the tender and delicate passion of love'. It does not occur to the hero that Cathrine was already pregnant before their marriage. Finding an excuse to leave for Edinburgh, Cathrine sends a note explaining that her doctor has advised her to stay in the city for the sake of following a medical 'regimen'. Not quite understanding this word, Richard wonders in horror, 'Shall his lady go and follow a regiment of common soldiers? — A horde of rude, vulgar, and beastly dogs?' He rushes to his bride's lodgings, calling out as he strides in, 'Is my wife here, or is she gone off with the soldiers?'

In the bedroom are the doctor, a lawyer, two maids, and Cathrine,

> sitting with a very young babe at her bosom, and weeping over it! I thought I should have sunk through the floor with astonishment, and it was long before I could speak another word. She was sitting up with some clothes around her, and held the child, which was a fine boy, on her two arms . . . . 'How's this, my dear?' says I. 'It's to be hoped that same baby is not yours?'
>
> She kept rocking the child as formerly, and weeping over it still more bitterly; but she neither lifted her eyes nor moved her tongue in answer to my question. My heart was like to melt; so I saw there was a necessity for rousing myself into a rage in order to preserve any little scrap of honour and dignity that remained to me. Accordingly, I turned to the doctor; and, tramping my foot violently on the floor, I said,

'There's for it now, sir! There's for it! That comes all of
your d—d prescriptions!'

'My prescriptions, Mr Rickleton?' said he, good-
humouredly. 'That boy came in consequence of my prescriptions, did you say? I beg you will consider, that I never
in my life prescribed for your lady till within these two
weeks'.

When I heard that, it struck me that the regiment business could hardly be made accountable for this sore calam-
ity, and that I must necessarily look elsewhere for some one
whereon to vent my just vengeance.

Knowing that Cathrine's former lover is a lawyer, Richard then
turns toward

the poor craven that stood gaping and trembling up in the
corner . . . for he was a very little spruce-looking handsome
fellow, if he had not been in such a panic. So I strode up to
him, and heaving my fist above his head, I vociferated into
his ear. 'I believe, sir, *you* are the man to whom I must look
for an explanation of this affair?'

'Mhoai, me, sir?' said he, rather flippantly, though in a
sad taking. 'Mhoai, as far as relates to what is law, sir —
mhoai, perhaps I may!'

'You then *are* a lawyer, sir?' said I, secure of my game.

'Mhoai, yes, sir, and a married gentleman like yourself',
said he.

Richard quickly agrees that no *married* man could have seduced
his wife. 'And now, sir', he adds, in a conciliatory tone,

'can you resolve me whether that boy can possibly be mine
or not? It is only a little better than three months since we
were married' . . . .

'Mhoai, sir, I believe', said the lawyer, 'that the child
being born in lawful wedlock, is yours in the eye of the law'.

'It strikes me that he has been forthcoming excessively
soon', says I.

'Mhoai, sir — Mhoai, that very often happens with the
first child', said the lawyer. 'But it very rarely ever happens

again; *Very* rarely, indeed. But, God bless you, sir! It is quite common with a woman's first child'.

Greatly comforted by this legal counsel, Richard wanders about the streets of Edinburgh in a confused state of mind and feeling 'as if I had been in a wilderness'. He is, he says, 'in need of some person to tell me the truth here, or tell me where it is to be found, for I can discover none of it save what is rolled up in a blanket'. He then learns that the lawyer is indeed the child's father, and, vowing vengeance, he unfortunately chases the wrong man to Glasgow, where he ends up in prison on a charge of assault. 'Whoy, after all, I must beg the gentleman's pardon', Richard pleads in court; 'I has been guilty of a foolish mistake'. Like his cousins in the preceding tale, Richard Rickleton enters the amorphous realm, confuses personal identity, and finally comes to admit that he himself is 'guilty', thus affirming his affinity with the rival. At length the hero forgets his pride, returns to Cathrine, and adopts her child as his own, adding, 'I never knew what social happiness was before'.

The third part of *The Three Perils of Woman* is a tragedy set in 1745. With savage irony Hogg will now demolish his old notion of the two journeys, implying in the process that *all* claims to superiority are illusions, in human life. The pedantic, lecherous clergyman of this tale will demonstrate, not just the relativity of conventional categories of good and evil, but the possibility of their complete inversion. The (unnamed) minister falls in love with his beautiful housekeeper, 'a flower in the very lowest walks of feminality', as he says, and plainly 'on the broad way that leadeth to destruction'. However, Sarah is strangely unappreciative towards this 'gentleman of my superlative qualifications, in all matters relating to intelligenciality', even though he offers to raise her 'to rank and high respect'. With himself and Sarah interned by the Jacobite army, the old man

> could no longer contain his jealousy, but followed her, calling her always to him, and reprimanding her at every turn. — 'Sarah, I say; come hither Sarah; come this way a little, Sarah. Where are you proceeding to, linked arm in arm with that young gentleman?'
>
> 'Oo, that's just a cousin o' mine, sir, that I haena seen for a long while'.

110

'Sarah, — what are you saying, Sarah? Are the Munroes
of Foulis your cousins, girl?'
'Oo, I daresay they ir, sir, — That young chield that's
waiting is my cousin ony how . . . '.

The basic theme of kinship is here brought to the surface through
the comic contrast between the self-important, analytical, judg-
mental clergyman, a man of discrete categories, and the free,
loving, irreverent Sarah, who knows that everyone is in effect her
'cousin' and that all people are 'gayan weel connected'.

Although he believes he is on the superior, ascending path, the
minister, like Gatty in the earlier story, is obviously embarked on
a descent. Set free after a major battle, he forgets about Sarah in
his haste to return home and protect his possessions. The
clergyman fails to see the symbolic implications of his 'tedious
journey over guns, bayonets, pistols' and corpses. He ignores the
cries of wounded and dying soldiers as he rides 'with full force,
half maddened by the injuries he supposed he had received' by
the theft of his property. Suddenly the horse stops, and, in an
image which mirrors the structure and essence of the whole story,
the minister finds himself 'flying in the air' before landing
unconscious on top of a corpse.

His life is saved by the blacksmith Peter Gow, who happens to
be Sarah's lover. The pastor immediately threatens to sue Peter,
demanding to know,

'Was there ever such a brutal thing heard of in a Christian
country as a minister of the gospel to be let blood of with a
horse-fleam, and his wound sewed up with a darning-needle,
and a thread twined of the hairs of a blacksmith? Oh you
unconscionable dog! Can any human frame overcome such
an operation?'
'Ay, and ten times more, sir. What is a fleam to a bayonet?
. . . '.

Hogg's satire repeatedly punctures the clergyman's categorical
outlook, undermines his pretensions to separateness and superiority, and stresses his involvement in the physical and animal
processes of normal human life. Later, again rebuffed by Sarah,
the old man dismisses her from his service. He refuses to pay the

111

five years' wages he owes her, claiming that a man of the cloth should be above such 'a morsel of filthy lucre'.

Meanwhile the minister's actions cause Peter Gow to think that Sarah has been unfaithful to him. Although he still loves her, Peter breaks off their engagement. Sarah then trudges north, without money, friends, or reputation, to begin a new life in the Highlands. She marries a Jacobite soldier named Alaster Mackenzie, just before the battle of Culloden. After the massacre Sarah tramps through the mountains to look for Alaster, seeing everywhere 'her husband's kinsmen and associates hanged up, and butchered in the most wanton manner as if for sport'. The descent into the unconscious by Gatty and Cherry, and Richard Rickleton's descent into confusion, is now parallelled by Sarah's horrifying journey through the scenes of war and persecution. At the same time her husband meets Peter Gow, and, spurred on by false gossip, the two jealous men fight each other in a duel. Each fatally wounds the other, but they live on for several days more. Sarah now joins the two dying men, explains that their suspicions 'had originated in mistake', and the three of them live together 'in the bonds of mutual affection' until Whig soldiers suddenly arrest and execute Peter and Alaster. Sarah becomes insane, and dies of exposure. The three young people have overcome rivalry and discovered fellowship, only to be destroyed in the end by realities outside their control. Throughout *The Three Perils of Woman*, Hogg's most unsettling and searching work, the author conveys his growing sense that literary symbols are inadequate to the complexity, unfairness, and potential tragedy of human life.

A torrent of critical outrage poured down upon the Shepherd after the publication of this novel in London, New York, and Paris. It was, the reviewers announced, 'profane and revolting to good feeling', while a few references to Edinburgh prostitutes were obviously 'in the worst possible taste'. Hogg was damned for his 'shockingly irreverent' tone, his 'coarseness and gross vulgarities', his 'sin' of 'overwhelming vulgarity', and his 'indecency, and even blasphemy'. His 'poverty of invention', another reader discovered, 'is in vain disguised by a thick coating of the most vulgar buffoonery'. John Wilson's review in *Blackwood's* was little more than a snobbish attack on the author's peasant origins, personality, and name: 'In one page, we listen to the song of the nightingale, and in another, to the grunt of the boar', Wilson

112

declared; 'Now the wood is vocal with the feathered choir; and then the sty bubbles and squeaks with a farm-sow, and a litter of nineteen pigwiggens'.

The small minority of critics who tried to find *aesthetic* values in *The Three Perils of Woman* took offence at Hogg's portrayal of changing, dynamic, and growing personalities. In real life, the reviewers explained, each person is endowed with a set, static, finite personality, largely determined by social position, whereas in Hogg's stories one could regrettably find 'the most inconsistent metamorphosis of character', with 'the whole drapery and costume . . . subject to alteration'. Hogg's heroines and heroes are too fluid, they 'want consistency and keeping', and so as a result 'we have such anomalies as the common jilting country servant girl of one chapter . . . acting the distinguished heroine of high sentiment and noble manners in another'.[30] Could these stultified reactions explain why Hogg's next major protagonist would be the absolutely stiff and static Robert Wringhim?

Notes

1   These details are taken from Blackwood's and Hogg's printed letters, 'To the Editor of the Glasgow Chronicle', 13 May 1818 (in NLS).
2   (Wilson), 'The Gander of Glasgow' (by 'Christopher North'), *Noctes Ambrosianae*, LV, *Blackwood's Magazine*, March 1831, pp. 568-70.
3   Scott, letter to the Duke of Buccleuch, 25 May (1818), printed in *The Letters of Sir Walter Scott*, ed. Grierson, 12 vols. (London, 1933), V, 154-55.
4   Hogg, letter to Scott, 3 Oct. 1821, printed in Strout, *The Life and Letters of James Hogg*, p. 227.
5   Anon. notices in *Newcastle Magazine*, Nov. 1829, p. 122; and *Scotsman*, 11 Nov. 1820, p. 199.
6   Hogg, *The Brownie of Bodsbeck*, ed. Douglas S. Mack (Edinburgh, 1976), p. 16.
7   Hogg, *The Brownie of Bodsbeck*, p. 119.
8   Hogg, *The Brownie of Bodsbeck*, p. 163.
9   Anon. revs. in *London Magazine*, June 1820, p. 667; *British Critic*, Oct. 1818, p. 412; *Literary Speculum*, II, 442; *Scotsman*, 16 May 1818, pp. 159, 158.
10 Hogg, 'The Wool-Gatherer', in his *Brownie of Bodsbeck; and Other Tales*, 2 vols. (Edinburgh and London, 1818), II, 89-228.
11 Anon. rev. in *Scotsman*, 16 May 1818, p. 159.

12 Hogg, 'The Battle of the Boyne', in *Forget Me Not* (London, 1832), pp. 299-304.

13 Hogg, 'Love Adventures of Mr George Cochrane', in his *Winter Evening Tales*, I, 217-303. This short novel is reprinted in *James Hogg: Tales of Love and Mystery*.

14 Anon. revs. in *London Magazine*, June 1820, p. 668; *Monthly Magazine*, July 1820, p. 555; *Blackwood's Magazine*, May 1820, pp. 149, 154; and *Scotsman*, 29 Apr. 1820, p. 143.

15 Hogg, 'Memoir', p. 54.

16 Letter to Allan Cunningham, 17 Oct. 1828, printed in R. B. Adam, *Works, Letters and Manuscripts of James Hogg* (Buffalo, 1930), p. 9.

17 Letter to Scott, printed in Norah Parr, *James Hogg at Home* (Dollar, 1980), p. 20.

18 Hogg, 'Memoir', p. 54.

19 Hogg, letter to Blackwood, 18 June 1830, printed in Parr, *James Hogg at Home*, p. 63.

20 Hogg, *The Three Perils of Man; War, Women and Witchcraft*, ed. Douglas Gifford (Edinburgh and London, 1972), p. 197.

21 Hogg, *The Three Perils of Man*, p. 151.

22 Hogg, *The Three Perils of Man*, p. 284.

23 A Cockney, *Scotch Novel Reading; or Modern Quackery; A Novel Really Founded on Facts*, 3 vols. (London, 1824), I, 10, and II, 111.

24 Hogg, *The Three Perils of Man*, p. 345.

25 C. S. Lewis, *The Allegory of Love: A Study of Medieval Tradition* (London, 1936), p. 314.

26 Hogg, *The Three Perils of Man*, p. 345.

27 Hogg, *The Three Perils of Man*, p. 346.

28 Hogg, *The Three Perils of Man*, p. 393.

29 Anon. revs. in *Monthly Review*, Aug. 1822, p. 440; *Literary Gazette*, 6 July 1822, pp. 419, 420; *Monthly Magazine*, Sept. 1822, p. 152; and *Literary Speculum*, II, 443.

30 Anon. revs. in *Literary Gazette*, 30 Aug. 1823, pp. 547, 548; *Repository of Modern Literature*, 2 vols. (London, 1823), II, 391; *Literary Chronicle*, 27 Sept. 1823, p. 615; *British Critic*, Oct. 1823, p. 361; *Blackwood's*, Oct. 1823, p. 427; *Emmet*, 18 Oct. 1823, p. 26; and *Literary Gazette*, 30 Aug. 1823, pp. 546, 548.

Chapter Six

CONFESSIONS OF AN ARTIST

THE August 1823 issue of *Blackwood's Magazine* carried a letter from James Hogg to 'Sir Christopher North', the fictional editor of its Noctes Ambrosianae series. The letter informs 'North' (a pseudonym for Hogg's sometime friend Professor Wilson) of an actual suicide's grave which had recently been dug up in Ettrick. Having been requested by North to write about 'the phenomena of nature', but finding 'no such phenomenons, if I understand that French word properly', the Shepherd offers, instead, this brief anecdote about a century-old corpse. Several questions arise, such as how the youth could have hanged himself with only a grass rope, and how his remains have survived intact for so long. Hogg ends by suggesting that North try the experiment of 'hang[ing] yourself in a hay rope, which, by the by, is to be made of risp, and leave orders that you are to be buried at a wild height', to ascertain whether, like the suicide's corpse, 'you shall set up your head at the last day as fresh as a moor-cock'.[1]

A year later James Hogg published his *Private Memoirs and Confessions of a Justified Sinner*. This, his finest work, is very much a poet's novel, relying for its deepest meanings on a combination of imagery, puns, allegory, structure, and the distinctive myth which Hogg was still exploring and developing.

The first half of the *Confessions*, together with a final postscript, is supposedly written by an 'editor' responding to the letter in *Blackwood's*. Almost everything about this editor, his arrogance, his modern upper-class Toryism, his friendship with other *Blackwood's* writers like Lockhart, and his university background, indicates that he is based on the real-life John Wilson, although in a few other respects he is a more generalised portrait of a successful man-of-letters. By gradually unveiling the pride, prejudices, and obtuseness of this 'editor', Hogg will enjoy a gleeful revenge on the critics, academics, and editors who dominated the literary world of the 1820's.

115

The main vehicle for this satire will be a series of precise parallels between the editor (a rationalist and man of the eighteenth century, in which he was born) and the second narrator (and protagonist), Robert Wringhim, a religious extremist and bigot and man of the seventeenth century. With consummate irony the novel will reveal deep affinities between its two antithetical narrators, one priding himself on his scientific and Enlightenment ideas, and the other proud of being 'a justified person',[2] one of God's chosen few.

On his side the editor is given to empirical phrases like 'the cause of the phenomenon',[3] Deistic catch-phrases like 'the Supreme Being' or 'the controller of Nature',[4] personified abstractions like 'Dame Reason' or 'the bosom of humanity',[5] and classical allusions such as 'Morphean measures' or 'the jovial party'.[6] His imagination is primarily spatial and visual; he paints a 'picture' of Robert's upbringing, assuring us that it is 'taken from nature and from truth'.[7] An Edinburgh riot becomes, through the editor's spectacles, more like a painting on canvas: 'A mob', he says, 'is like a spring-tide in an eastern storm, that retires only to return with more overwhelming fury'.[8] His lofty, expansive rhetoric helps him to distance himself from the confusion of life, to impose order on a world that (as Hogg is always trying to show) fundamentally lacks order.

A similar desire to tame the chaos motivates Robert Wringhim. If the editor strives for detachment and perspective, backed by his 'powerful monitors'[9] of history and tradition, Wringhim strives for superiority through his sense of passionate commitment backed by 'the might of heaven'.[10] In his writing he seeks to control reality through Calvinist catch-phrases like 'absolute predestination' or 'the covenant of promise',[11] by repeatedly stressing the first person singular, by avoiding abstract thought, and through numerous Biblical allusions. Unlike his opposite number Robert scorns visual images and pictorial representation. His obsession is with the word and with dogma. His eye is almost always on himself: 'My life has been a life of trouble and turmoil', he begins; 'I was born an outcast in the world, in which I was destined to act so conspicuous a part'.[12]

Each of the two narrators in the *Confessions* has a kind of 'double', a mysterious mirror-image whose presence tempts him further along the descending path into confusion. Robert's double, his doppelganger Gil-Martin, strangely resembles Robert himself, whom Gil-Martin will entice to commit murder in order to fulfil God's plan by 'cut[ting] off the enemies of the Lord from the face of the earth'.[13] On the other hand the editor's double is Robert, who strangely resembles the editor, and whose autobiography will entice the editor to embark on a similar descent.

Although the *Confessions* has a universal and modern significance that makes it popular with many readers around the world, it is also very deeply rooted in the traditions and history of southern Scotland. As in *The Brownie of Bodsbeck*, the *Confessions* explores the outlook of seventeenth-century extreme Presbyterians, who held the predestinarian doctrine that salvation was entirely the gift of God rather than something which could be merited by the efforts of an individual. At first sight the *Confessions* seems the very opposite of the *Brownie*, in its satirical presentation of a single-minded Calvinist who first murders a moderate clergyman (named, suggestively, Reverend Blanchard), and then goes on to commit fratricide, perjury, and other crimes, all under the impression that he is one of God's favourite people, that his sins will be overlooked, and that in any event everything on earth has been pre-arranged or predestined by God. Robert Wringhim's twisted Calvinism is shown to be mainly self-interested since it permits him to kill his enemies, inherit the estate of Dalcastle, and perceive himself as spiritually superior to other people. Yet in choosing a deluded, hypocritical extremist for his protagonist, Hogg has something in common with Thomas Boston, a preacher whose famous book *Human Nature, in its Four-fold State* had attempted to forge a more reflective interpretation of Calvinism within the Church of Scotland. Minister in Ettrick until his death in 1732, the son of Covenanter parents, Boston had been well acquainted with people like Robert, 'who, when once they had gathered some scraps of knowledge of religion . . . do swell big with *conceit* of themselves'. The human soul, according to Boston, experiences four distinct stages or conditions: a state of Primitive Integrity, a state of Nature (or Entire Deprivation), a state of Grace (or Begun Recovery), and finally an Eternal State. In the second category, man is completely depraved, has no freedom, and can 'do nothing but sin'; it is in this second state (if Boston's categories can be accepted for a moment) that Robert Wringhim surely belongs, in spite of his loud pretensions to holiness. The third state, that of Begun Recovery, is apparently characterised by 'a fixed *aversion* to evil', a desire for self-improvement, and a sense of 'mystical union',[14] none of which is felt by Robert.

James Hogg definitely did not share Thomas Boston's puritanical distrust of nature, but he was familiar with the *Four-fold State*, which enjoyed great popularity until well into the nineteenth century. The *Confessions*, however, is a novel, not a statement of doctrine, and it achieves balance and profound ambiguity by depicting Robert Wringhim both ironically and (to some extent) sympathetically. By telling the same story twice, from the editor's point-of-view and from Robert's point-of-view, Hogg is once again looking at the dichotomy between objectivity and subjectivity. His *Confessions*, like his *Brownie of Bodsbeck*, exposes the inhumanity of narrow-minded religion, yet at the same time asserts the humanity and deep misfortune of the individuals who become trapped within those doctrines.

The editor's rationalism is certainly an improvement over Wringhim's perversion of religion, but Hogg's purpose is evidently to show that each of the two narrators is the product of his times and his society, and to find similarities underneath their very diverse temperaments. It is fitting that the editor's limitations should be less apparent, less horrible in result, and yet equal in kind, with those of his counterpart. Deceit is obvious on every page of Robert's account, and he is, as he admits, 'particularly prone to lying'.[15] For all his pride in objectivity, the editor is equally capable of dishonesty, as we discover when he and his friends enlist a local guide to help them find the hero's grave:

> We got a fine old shepherd, named W——m B——e, a great original, and a very obliging and civil man, who asked no conditions but that we should not speak of it, because he did not wish it to come to his master's ears, that he had been engaged in *sic a profane thing*. We promised strict secrecy; and . . . proceeded to the grave.[16]

The editor, in this crucial passage, is as much a liar as Robert Wringhim. He clearly has no intention of keeping the promise of 'strict secrecy' with which he tricks this 'obliging and civil man', since immediately on returning to the city the editor will complete his manuscript and send it down to London for publication.

Each writer employs distinctive and contrasting techniques for denying otherness and forestalling any effective challenge to his received ideas. Anyone who disagrees with Robert is automatically classified with 'the wicked and profane'.[17] When his brother disputes the Calvinist theory of predestination, Robert replies,

But why should I wonder at such abandoned notions and principles? It was fore-ordained that you should cherish them, and that they should be the ruin of your soul and body, before the world was framed.[18]

Equally circumscribed by opposite preconceptions, the editor dismisses Robert's mother's prayers, on her wedding-night, as merely 'the cant of the bigot or the hypocrite' against which 'no reasoning can aught avail',[19] even though the unfortunate bride is far from being the hardened zealot she later becomes. The editor is a high-handed, close-minded Tory, rudely excluding his old shepherd guide B——e in referring to the 'four respectable witnesses'[20] at Robert's grave, and breezily contrasting 'the free principles cherished by the [Royalist] court party' with those of 'their severe and carping contemporaries'.[21] He closely resembles Robert in being incapable of genuinely contemplating alternative perspectives. Dismissive phrases such as 'the rage of fanaticism'[22] protect him from having to question the real causes of disunity, just as, on the other side of the fence, Robert Wringhim speaks of 'the unregenerate' or 'the wicked of this land'[23] to stigmatise those whose point-of-view differs from his own. Despite one man's pretense of objectivity, and the other's pretense of pure, divinely-sanctioned subjectivity, they each remain locked within their own personal illusions of superiority. They are united by their distrust of shared reality and their impulse to separate themselves from natural and social processes.

The unconscious kinship between the editor and Robert is superbly dramatised in the last pages of each account, when each respective writer leaves his private study and goes on a long, confusing, discouraging journey. What the editor looks forward to as a pleasant holiday turns, in both a geographic and a spiritual or psychological sense, into a comic, burlesque version of Robert's tragic flight. Riding to Edinburgh and through the Lowlands to inspect the suicide's grave, the editor never stops to consider that his roundabout route in 1823 is almost identical to the one that brought Wringhim to his death in 1712. Robert must travel in disguise to avoid being arrested, while the editor, anxious to gain the respect of the Borderers, appears in Ettrick in the unconvincing guise of a wholesale wool-buyer. Just as one writer loses his *religious* certainty near the end, the other loses his *rationalistic* certainty, doubting the veracity of his own research and wondering if he has come to the right grave. The editor's despair at not finding a logical solution to the story he has worked on, his unwillingness to 'bid any rational being' to credit a tale 'so far out of the common course',[24] is an appropriate analogy to Robert Wringhim's increasing fears about his own chances of salvation as he draws closer and closer to committing suicide.

The ending of each narrative section subverts the individualism of the two writers by emphasising their similarities, reducing them to the same level of confusion and self-doubt, and showing their involvement in relationship, process, and community. The narrators end in despair, but a perceptive reader may complete their journeys by recalling previous works by James Hogg, or by listening to the strongly implied affirmation of social vision and fellowship in the final pages, as Robert and the editor are increasingly helped by, and at the mercy of, the shepherds, farmers, weavers, and other unpretentious inhabitants of Ettrick Forest. 'I was made welcome in every house', writes Robert; 'We went into a shepherd's cot to get a drink of milk',[25] writes the editor.

The *Confessions* achieves through irony and structure what several Romantic poems, such as *The Ancient Mariner* and *Prometheus Unbound*, assert more directly. Hogg, too, first leads the reader into a fluid or nightmare realm of melting personal identities, where for instance Robert discovers, 'Either I had a second self . . . or else my body was at times possessed by a spirit'.[26] Robert and the editor of course fall victim to this lower world, yet at the end Hogg finds subtle ways of pointing the reader on the path of escape, the upward path towards the recovery of personal wholeness and spiritual re-birth through the necessary acceptance of the oneness of humanity.

Few readers have given the *Confessions* the careful re-reading it deserves. Lovers of detective fiction should be able to solve at least some of its mysteries, such as the real (and quite surprising) identity of Lawyer Linkum, who is not a lawyer at all, and whose legal documents are entirely bogus, although presumably these are among the old registers used by the editor as the basis of his scientific research. Lawyer Linkum links the two halves of the novel and brings a better balance between the two narrators. Not only do his fabrications drastically undercut the editor's vaunted objectivity, but they also indicate clearly that Wringhim is innocent of some of the charges against him, such as fraud and forgery. A closer look at the role of 'Linkum' in *both* halves of the *Confessions* will arouse greater sympathy for Robert Wringhim, who, however evil and self-stupefied he becomes, is also a victim of his environment, and a victim of Gil-Martin, Linkum, Ridsley, and (much later) the editor. Robert is no cardboard villain, but an extreme version of Everyman, a human character with symbolic and universal implications for every reader.

The theme of the novel is the relativity of the human self, which is shown to be a function of time, process, nature, and society. Neither narrator dreams of looking for universal or common significance underlying his experience, and each is therefore doomed to be a victim, a hard kernel of absolute selfhood crushed by external forces. Robert, sealed up in his repressive theology, always sees himself as the superior, autonomous soul, unaltered by time and essentially independent of relationship; the editor, though more complex, modern, and sophisticated, is equally self-satisfied, self-righteous, stiff, and unchanging. Each follows the descending path from arrogance down into the physical and further down into extreme uncertainty, but neither man notices the pattern or makes the final leap from despair to fellowship and renewed purpose.

A deeper balance is also achieved in the *Confessions* through what Robert calls 'a thousand interminable quibbles'.[27] These countless puns and quibbles create a wider, ironic perspective which implicitly transcends the puritanism of one narrator and the supposed Enlightenment of the other. After his first meeting with Gil-Martin, Robert writes happily, 'I was quite captivated';[28] this statement expresses the hero's fascination with his new friend, and also goes to the heart of the novel in foreshadowing his actual physical as well as spiritual enslavement, when he will be literally 'led away captive'.[29] When Robert tries to make friends in

121

his last days by pretending to be 'a poor student of theology',[30] his words are again true in a way that he does not suspect.

Time after time Robert becomes the victim of his own words. When Gil-Martin says, 'You have a father and a brother according to the flesh, what do you know of them?' he replies pompously and forlornly, 'I am sorry to say I know nothing good'.[31] He does indeed 'know nothing good', both in the limited way he uses that phrase, and in the wider sense of having cut himself off from 'the good' through restrictive religion, elitism, and acts of murder. The fact that Wringhim often utters double meanings without recognising them indicates his narrowed vision, his fragmented personality, and his lack of self-knowledge. Ironic puns repeatedly point out the difference between Robert's partial outlook and James Hogg's more complex, irreducible, and mature outlook on life. On learning that he is one of God's favourite people, Robert is also pleased to hear the prediction, '[Y]our reward shall be double'[32] — as indeed it will be, in more ways than two.

These puns, and many more like them, convey a joyful intuition of unity underneath the surface of language and the surface of life. Like the many symbols and allegories of Hogg's poetry, they ask readers to find connections between conventionally opposite categories like the natural, social, and spiritual. In a similar vein is the response to a burglary in her house by a young servant, who gives a sexual meaning to words her mistress employs in a purely economic sense: 'When we got the candle lightit', she recalls,

> a' the house was in a hoad-road. 'Bessy, my woman' [said
> the mistress], 'we are baith ruined and undone creatures.'
> 'The deil a bit' [answered Bessy]; 'that I deny positively.
> H'mh! to speak o' a lass o' my age being ruined and undone!
> I never had muckle except what was within a good jerkin
> [i.e., prophylactic], an' let the thief ruin me there wha can'.[33]

The best of all the double meanings comes in the last pages of Robert's diary. 'And to what I am now reduced', he writes in his misery, 'let the reflecting reader judge'.[34] The 'reflecting' reader is none other than Robert's latter-day counterpart, his 1820's mirror-image the editor, the man who will first read Robert's manuscript, and *reflect* or mirror Robert's descent into chaos. Like the grave-robbing, ring-snatching monk of *Pilgrims of the*

Sun, the editor is Hogg's portrait of a poor reader or critic; he never sees the parallels between himself and the protagonist, and so he never profits from Robert's implied warning. Despite his earnest claim that 'no person, man or woman, will ever peruse [Robert's journal] with the same attention that I have done',[35] this meticulous reader finds only single meanings instead of double meanings and he too is 'reduced' in the final 'reflecting' pages of the novel.

Thanks to their mind-forged manacles of divisive religion or divisive rationalism, the two narrators are prisoners of language, victims of the closed systems of discourse they blindly impose upon reality. It is only the artist James Hogg, and his perceptive readers, who enjoy a freedom with words, and a more unified vision of life, by glimpsing double meanings, double narratives, and double journeys.

A central symbol in the *Confessions* is the image of the net or web. This appears as a tennis net when Robert pretends to be 'king of the game',[36] as a make-shift net with which two women later tie Robert's 'hands behind his back, and his feet fast with long strips of garters',[37] and as a large weaver's loom which Robert falls into in the dark. 'I wanted to be at the light', he cries to the owner, 'and have somehow unfortunately involved myself in the intricacies of your web'.[38] The loom symbolises the strands of doctrine which Wringhim tries to foist upon other people, and in which he himself comes to be trapped.

The net or web also symbolises the perspectivism that has been a feature of Hogg's work since *The Queen's Wake*, and which may be seen in the several narratives of his *Perils*, and now in the two sections of the *Confessions*. Walking in a mist at sunrise, Robert's brother George has a benign vision of this web when he notices that his hat is 'all covered with a tissue of the most delicate silver — a fairy web, composed of little spheres, so minute that no eye could discern any one of them; yet there they were shining in lovely millions'.[39] George's beaver hat is a round object symbolically uniting human, natural, and supernatural, like the 'rings' of Hogg's long poems. Its 'fairy web, composed of little spheres', brings a moment of epiphany to George, who for a moment penetrates the mist to see kaleidoscopic unity, pattern, and purpose. Although confusion remains the inescapable condition of human life, Robert's brother breaks through that state, and momentarily transcends the limitations of individual perspective by sensing wholeness and form.

A good reader will approach the *Confessions* as a work of art, finding form and meaning in the web of words, rather than becoming trapped in that web like the two narrators. From this more aesthetic standpoint its two parallel journeys reveal Hogg's characteristic movement from individualism to community. There is also, in an abstract or formal way, a carry-over from his old idea of a ring formed by two paths, with Robert tracing an upward parabola through tragedy, and the editor following a downward arc as the victim of a comedy. This ring or cycle can be seen as Hogg's symbolic answer to the one-dimensionality of Robert's vertical outlook, and the editor's horizontal outlook.

James Hogg would not have agreed with Robert Wringhim about ethics or religion, but still there are striking similarities between the author and his protagonist. Robert's claim to being divinely-sanctioned can be put beside the author's 'conviction that a heavenly gift, conferring the powers of immortal song, was inherent in my soul'.[40] Following in a long poetical tradition, Hogg spoke of 'the talent which God had given me',[41] and pictured himself as being, through his art, a 'candidate for immortal fame'. In 1812 he felt 'an inward consciousness that I should yet live to be compared with Burns', although the minister who heard this confession 'mortified' the young poet (a little like Gil-Martin embarrassing Robert) by repeating his assertion 'as a bitter jest against me in a party that same evening'. His belief in his own 'transcendent poetical genius' would inevitably alienate Hogg from society and from prevailing literary standards, so that like his protagonist he often stood utterly alone in his judgments. '[A]las! for my unfortunate Pilgrim!' wrote Hogg, after his *Pilgrims of the Sun* met with hostile criticism; his friend John Grieve, however, 'checked me, by saying it was impossible that I could be a better judge than both the literary people of Scotland and England'.[42]

The Shepherd would have been well aware of some similarities between his own conviction of being an inspired author, and Wringhim's more extreme claim of being God's direct representative. One very revealing poem recalls Hogg's childhood days when, alone on the hills of Ettrick, he felt in an 'ecstasy'[43]

That at the leap, the race, or the throw,
Or tuneful lay of the greenwood glen,
I was the chief of the sons of men.

Fortunately for James Hogg, however, he soon learned to view 'this conceit' from a more objective point-of-view, and to direct his 'high resolve' towards useful goals. Yet even as an adult he continued to believe in the underlying intuition as a defense against conformism:

—Without resolve that mocks controul,
A conscious energy of soul
That views no height to human skill,
Man never excelled and never will.

Hogg never surrendered to the conventional standards of his day, but on the other hand, unlike Robert Wringhim, he was able to respond creatively to criticism, to use art as a form of dialogue with his society, and to grow by adjusting to challenge, just as the poet in *The Queen's Wake* eventually learns to admit adversity, to accept the wind and the storm. In doing so, Hogg exchanges the vertical conception of art as a divine mission, for a more humane, more cyclical understanding which recognises the artist's involvement in, dependence upon, and responsibility to, his society and his times.

Just as Robert pretends to be a passive agent of God's will, James Hogg often felt that his imagination derived from a superior source which was beyond his conscious control. Many times Hogg claimed to be inspired by a spontaneous creative force, a 'fire and rapidity of true genius'.[44] '[W]hen I write the first line of a tale or novel I know not what the second is to be', he declared, 'and it is the same way in every sentence throughout'.[45] This is very different from Robert's crazy phantasy of being one of God's chosen murderers, yet to some extent his hero's self-image is an objective correlative to Hogg's own self-image as a writer. Writing the *Confessions* may well have been therapeutic, a chance to objectify his own literary struggles, warn himself against the dangers of becoming static or self-enclosed, and even laugh at himself. 'After my literary blunders and miscarriages are

125

a few months old', he once confessed, 'I can view them with as much indifference, and laugh at them as heartily, as any of my neighbours'. There is, of course, a great deal of high-spirited self-mockery in Hogg's implied analogy between the artist and the murderer. It is also necessary to keep in mind the Shepherd's symbolic and catholic attitude towards religion, as well as the widely-held Romantic theory of artistic creativity as a gift from the gods.

Many critics have noticed the way that Robert Wringhim's ambivalent relationship with Gil-Martin is very similar to Hogg's experience in the *Blackwood's* group. Hogg frequently claimed that William Blackwood 'had driven me beyond the bounds of human patience', or that 'That Magazine of his' had 'put words and sentiments into my mouth of which I have been greatly ashamed'.[46]

At times *Blackwood's* would declare the Shepherd an immortal poet, 'deathless'[47] as Shakespeare, while at other times painting him as 'the greatest boar on earth', a 'lout . . . enveloped in a coarse plaid impregnated with tobacco, with a prodigious mouth-ful of immeasurable tusks, and a dialect that set all conjecture at defiance'.[48] Gil-Martin's attentions to Robert are analogous to the combination of encouragement and condescension which Hogg received from many Edinburgh men-of-letters, whose aggressive intellects were often a torment to him. Lockhart, for instance, according to Dr Browne, made Hogg 'a continual butt for raillery and derision, cramming him with all manner of nonsense and absurdity, and literally laughing in the face of the poor gudgeon', while 'doubtless sniggering in his sleeve at the idea of *such* a protégé'.[49] And, like Wringhim, James Hogg was often ambivalent and sometimes expressed bitter feelings of exclusion and persecution:

I know that I have always been looked on by the learned part of the community as an intruder in the paths of litera-ture, and every opprobrium has been thrown on me from that quarter. The truth is, that I am so. The walks of learn-ing are occupied by a powerful aristocracy, who deem that province their own peculiar right; else, what would avail all their dear-bought collegiate honours and degrees? No won-der that they should view an intruder, from the humble and despised ranks of the community, with a jealous and indignant eye, and impede his progress by every means in their power.

Robert's ambition of seeing his diary in print places him in the power of the demons, and, metaphorically, so did Hogg's desire for publication put James Hogg at the mercy of 'demons'. The devils who plague Wringhim as he adds the finishing touches to his journal might be compared with the 'printer's devils' (a common phrase of the 1820's to describe typesetters) with whom both he, and his creator James Hogg, were familiar. In his *Spy* days for example the Shepherd would often go 'down to a dark house in the Cowgate, where we drank whisky and ate rolls with a number of printers, the dirtiest and leanest-looking men I had ever seen'. Once a work was published a critic might act like 'a malicious *deevil*', while Hogg's prim women readers sometimes seemed to him like 'Gaping deevils'.[50]

Robert Wringhim is quite literally 'justified' (another printing term) when, in Edinburgh, he supervises the printer's devils in setting up his Memoirs in 'justified' type. By the same token James Hogg would become a 'justified sinner' each time his prose works appeared in print. The Calvinist concepts of election and justification had also become an in-joke which could be applied to any author seeking public favour; even Francis Jeffrey could predict, after *The Queen's Wake*, that Hogg 'is yet doomed to justify his early election'[51] as an author.

Hogg's literary career, like Wringhim's, was a difficult journey through a hostile world. Both writers offended against social conventions, and Wringhim's crimes have their milder parallel in some of Hogg's questionable dealings with publishers and creditors. When one former publisher charged him with 'a propensity to falsehood, and a meanness of soul quite inexplicable', Hogg defended his conduct and threatened to 'see the firm of Oliver & Boyd and the dog Goldie d—d to hell'.[52] A little like Robert Wringhim (but in a very different way) Hogg in his writing often upset moralistic or pious readers, so that one disgruntled critic could announce that with 'heaven-daring, and altogether unparalleled temerity', the Ettrick Shepherd had actually presumed to 'set himself over the Shepherd of Israel', thus audaciously turning himself into practically 'the Pope of the Border'.[53] Hogg's lesser 'sins', those 'indelicacies hinted at by some reviewers', may also be compared with Robert's crimes; 'All that I can say for myself', admitted Hogg in later years, 'is, that I am certain I never intentionally meant ill, and that I hope to be forgiven, both by God and man'.[54]

Robert is a poor writer, locked in his intense subjectivity and therefore unable to progress from despair through to fellowship. He experiences (but without ever understanding) many of the hard lessons which shaped the artistic growth of James Hogg: the relativity of social bonds, of moral attitudes, and of the self, the necessary schism between artistic vision and social realities, and the tremendous power of society over its writers. Like those foolish bards in *The Poetic Mirror*, or the bishop of 'The Gude Greye Katt', Robert can only travel part of the distance. Hogg leaves him hanging in a hayfield, just as the flying cat leaves her bishop inside a volcano.

The *Confessions* is one of several works in which Hogg uses the journey as an image both of life and of the creative process. In his 'Seeking the Houdy' he again writes about writing, this time through the metaphor of a shepherd who rides to fetch the houdy (or mid-wife). The first half of this tale is in genteel, correct English, which corresponds to the slowness of Robin and his horse. The second half, after a witch has climbed onto the horse behind the shepherd, is mainly in the Scots language, which brings new energy to the horse and (evidently) to James Hogg. With the witch behind him the shepherd has

> no other shift left, than to fix by instinct on the mane wi' baith hands, an' cry out to the mare to stop. 'Wo ye auld viper o' the pit! wo, ye beast o' Bashan!' I cries in outer desperation; but ay the louder I cried, the faster did the glyde flee. She snored, an' she grained, an' she reirdit baith ahint an' afore; an' on she dashed, regardless of a' danger.
>
> I soon lost sight o' the ground — off gaed my bonnet, an' away i' the wind — off gaed my plaid, an' away i' the wind; an' there was I sitting lootching forret, cleaving the wind like an arrow out of a bow, an' my een rinning pouring like streams of water from the south. At length we came to the Birk-bush Linn! and alangst the very verge of that awsome precipice there was my dementit beast scouring like a fiery

dragon. 'Lord preserve me!' cried I loud out; an' I hadna weel said the word, till my mare gae a tremendous plunge . . . .[55]

At this juncture the witch flies off the horse and 'ower the precipice' 'like a shot stern'. The two halves of this story recall the *Confessions*, with the first part in a rational, proper, restrained style, and the second half impetuous, instinctive, and impelled by a love of local legends, folk traditions, and the supernatural.

Hogg returns to his theory of the creative experience in 'Eastern Apologues'. The hero, a one-armed, one-legged peasant, lectures his monarch on 'the gift of song',[56] which, he explains, is 'an emanation from the Deity', a 'sublime intellectual radiance', and a 'holy flame that poured from the mouths of Moses, of David, of Isaiah, and of Mahomed'. The peasant Ismael then recites his parable about an ox and a goat. The two animals come to a deserted city, where the ox, gorging on the rich grapes and other delicacies, soon becomes too fat to escape through the city gates. Trapped by his obesity, the ox is easily killed by hunters, while the goat, more moderate and energetic, skips away to the forest for safety. The goat has a vitality and love of motion which allows him (like James Hogg) to survive difficult times, to travel between town and country, to adjust to changing conditions, and to explore different perspectives; 'he would gambol among the flowers, and butt down the young vines and olives as with disdain, and then, bounding over the fences, escape into the forest again'. By contrast, the ox might represent any number of authors who, in Hogg's view, have become static or overly concerned with merely physical, material, or economic aspects of life.

I have tried to show that James Hogg marks out the main sections of his metaphorical path through certain favourite images, such as a pool of water, a storm or battle, a duel, a web, and, near the end, either a grave, a wedding, or a birth. Similar recurring signposts would include the teacher, the lawyer, the doctor, a dog or pig or other animal, and, most importantly, the void, which first appears in Cherry's dream in *The Three Perils of Woman*, and remains a major image in later journeys. Robert Wringhim is 'hung by the locks over a yawning chasm, to which I could perceive no bottom',[57] and the shepherd of 'Seeking the Houdy' is likewise brought to 'the very verge of that awsome

129

precipice'.The best example of Hogg's use of the void occurs in 'The First Sermon', when an apprentice preacher loses the thread of his sermon:

> The *hems!* and *haws!* began to come more close;
> Three at a time! The cambric handkerchief
> Came greatly in request. The burly head
> Gave over tossing. The fine cheek grew red —
> Then pale — then blue — then to a heavy crimson!
> . . . .
> In every line his countenance bespoke
> The loss of recollection; all within
> Became a blank — a chaos of confusion,
> Producing nought but agony of soul.
> His long lip quiver'd, and his shaking hand
> Of the trim beaver scarcely could make seizure,
> When, stooping, floundering, plaiting at the knees,
> He — made his exit.[58]

This passage intriguingly echoes an experience of the young Mr Spy, as well as recalling Cherry's embarrassing loss-of-consciousness in the church in *The Three Perils of Woman*. The would-be minister falls into the horrible hollowness 'within'; he sees that his mind is 'a blank — a chaos of confusion' which gives 'nought' except 'agony of soul'. As in the *Confessions*, a proud, egotistical man of religion is ironically paired with an equally proud but rationalistic, Anglicised, and complacent narrator, who merely laughs at the youth's downfall:

> As for myself,
> I laugh'd till I was sick; went home to dinner,
> Drank the poor preacher's health, and laugh'd again.

Both characters make a hasty retreat from the void, the narrator by withdrawing to a good dinner and uttering fatuous comments about what 'I have oft bethought me it were best', while the young man goes

> home to his own native kingdom — Fife,
> Pass'd to his father's stable — seized a pair
> Of strong plough-bridle reins, and hang'd himself.

130

Like the *Confessions*, Hogg's 'First Sermon' requires us to see underlying parallels between opposite personality types, to discover the theme of community, and to complete the last leg of the journey ourselves.

Notes

1 Hogg, 'A Scots Mummy: To Sir Christopher North', *Blackwood's Magazine*, Aug. 1823, pp. 188-90.
2 Hogg, *The Private Memoirs and Confessions of a Justified Sinner*, ed. John Carey (London, 1969), p. 115.
3 Hogg, *Confessions*, p. 40.
4 Hogg, *Confessions*, pp. 16, 56.
5 Hogg, *Confessions*, pp. 51, 69.
6 Hogg, *Confessions*, pp. 6, 51.
7 Hogg, *Confessions*, pp. 16-17.
8 Hogg, *Confessions*, p. 28.
9 Hogg, *Confessions*, p. 1.
10 Hogg, *Confessions*, p. 97.
11 Hogg, *Confessions*, pp. 123, 102.
12 Hogg, *Confessions*, p. 97.
13 Hogg, *Confessions*, p. 122.
14 Boston, *Human Nature, in its Four-fold State* (1720; 15th. ed., rev., Glasgow, 1761), pp. 21, 109, 190, 233.
15 Hogg, *Confessions*, p. 108.
16 Hogg, *Confessions*, p. 247.
17 Hogg, *Confessions*, p. 172.
18 Hogg, *Confessions*, p. 44.
19 Hogg, *Confessions*, p. 5.
20 Hogg, *Confessions*, p. 249.
21 Hogg, *Confessions*, p. 2.
22 Hogg, *Confessions*, p. 93.
23 Hogg, *Confessions*, p. 150.
24 Hogg, *Confessions*, p. 240.
25 Hogg, *Confessions*, pp. 236, 247.
26 Hogg, *Confessions*, p. 182. The Romantic context is discussed in my article, 'James Hogg's *Confessions* and the Vale of Soul-Making', in *Studies in Scottish Fiction: Nineteenth Century*, ed. Horst W. Drescher and Joachim Schwend (Frankfurt: Lang, 1985), pp. 29-41.
27 Hogg, *Confessions*, p. 193.
28 Hogg, *Confessions*, p. 118.
29 Hogg, *Confessions*, p. 233.
30 Hogg, *Confessions*, p. 230.
31 Hogg, *Confessions*, p. 145.
32 Hogg, *Confessions*, p. 115.

33 Hogg, *Confessions*, p. 66.
34 Hogg, *Confessions*, pp. 238-39.
35 Hogg, *Confessions*, pp. 253-54.
36 Hogg, *Confessions*, p. 21.
37 Hogg, *Confessions*, p. 89.
38 Hogg, *Confessions*, p. 215.
39 Hogg, *Confessions*, p. 39.
40 Hogg, 'Memoir', p. 54.
41 Hogg, 'Familiar Anecdotes of Sir Walter Scott', p. 124.
42 Hogg, 'Memoir', pp. 41, 12, 67, 36.
43 Hogg, 'The Minstrel Boy', *Friendship's Offering* (1829), pp. 209-13.
44 Hogg, *A Series of Lay Sermons* (London, 1834), p. 274.
45 Hogg, 'Familiar Anecdotes of Sir Walter Scott', p. 101.
46 Hogg, 'Memoir', pp. 33, 59.
47 Gillies, 'Sonnet: On Seeing a Spark fall from Mr Hogg's Pipe', *Blackwood's Magazine*, May 1819, p. 205.
48 An Old Friend with a New Face, 'On Hogg's Memoirs', *Blackwood's Magazine*, Aug. 1821, p. 43.
49 *'Life' of the Ettrick Shepherd Anatomized*, p. 4.
50 Hogg, 'Memoir', pp. 46, 20, 41, 20.
51 Anon. rev., in *Edinburgh Review*, Nov. 1814, p. 160.
52 George Goldie, *Letter to a Friend in London* (Edinburgh, 1821), and Hogg, letter to Oliver & Boyd, 24 June 1821, both rpt. in Douglas Mack's Commentary to Hogg's *Memoir of the Author's Life and Familiar Anecdotes of Sir Walter Scott*, pp. 88-89.
53 T. Friendly, *The Pope of the Border; or, a Word of Reproof, in a Letter to James Hogg, the Etterick Shepherd* (Edinburgh, 1834), pp. 3, 6.
54 Hogg, 'Memoir', p. 50.
55 Hogg, 'Seeking the Houdy', *Forget-me-Not* (1830), pp. 399-413. This tale, together with 'Eastern Apologues' and 'The First Sermon', is reprinted in *James Hogg: Tales of Love and Mystery*.
56 Hogg, 'Eastern Apologues', *Forget-me-Not* (1829), pp. 309-23.
57 Hogg, *Confessions*, p. 239.
58 Hogg, 'The First Sermon', *Blackwood's Magazine*, June 1830, pp. 879-80.

Chapter Seven

A GREAT
PARACENTRICAL PARABOLA

[Phrenology] can alone account for such men as Hogg.
Certain of his organs are splendidly developed, and others as
miserably. This explains the fine imagination, and lamen-
table want of sense, which this strange compound of genius
and imbecility — of strength and weakness — so oddly
exhibits.[1]

THE *Confessions* was not well received. And, although the novel
was published anonymously, its veil was soon stripped away to
reveal the guilty author. 'Write what he will, there is a diseased
and itching peculiarity of style, a *scabies et porrigo Porci*, which',
opined one reviewer, 'is always sure to betray Mr Hogg'. Hogg's
prestige fell rapidly during the 1820's, partly as a result of the
Blackwood's caricature, and partly because of his superb *Perils*
and *Confessions*. Jeremy Bentham's *Westminster Review* found his
work 'inspired by insolence and whisky-punch', 'an experiment
intended to ascertain how far the English public will allow itself to
be insulted', while Leigh Hunt's *Examiner* complained of a
'surprising lack of probability, or even possibility'. In Glasgow
The Emmet wondered pathetically why the Shepherd 'had left his
own sweet little land of poetry, and come into contact with the
bodily animals of this sluggish earth, of whose characters and
manners he held up a daubish and distorted view'. '[H]ear the
gross Hogg how he bellows',[2] commented another critic. With
publishers growing wary Hogg relied increasingly on the short
pieces he could still peddle to the Christmas annuals and to a
small circle of journals in Edinburgh, Newcastle, London, Belfast
and Dublin.

In public James Hogg often seemed to be trying his hardest to
offend upper-class book-buyers. The Irish poet Tom Moore once
went with Scott, Wilson and Jeffrey to a literary dinner where

Hogg 'yelled out savagely two or three Scotch songs, and accompanied the burden of one of them by labouring away upon the bare shoulders of the ladies who sat on each side of him'.[3] Another account of this banquet tells us that 'two peeresses' had begged to be invited, only to arrive

> in full evening costume, or, as Moore described it, 'in shoulders'. When supper was half over, James Hogg, the Ettrick Shepherd, appeared. A chair had been designedly left vacant for him between the two aristocrats. His approach was discernible before his person was visible; for he came straight from a cattle fair, and was reeking with the unsavoury odours of the sheep and pigs and oxen, in whose company he had been for hours. Nevertheless he soon made himself at home with the fair ladies on each side of him: somewhat too much so, for, supper over, the cloth withdrawn, and the toddy introduced, the song going round, and his next door neighbours being too languid in their manner of joining in the chorus to please him, he turned first to the right hand, then to the left, and slapped both of them on their backs with such good will as to make their blade bones ring again; then, with a yell of an Ojibbaway Indian, he shouted forth, 'Noo then, leddies, follow me! Heigh tutti, tutti! Heigh tutti, tutti!!'[4]

How would this marvellous and free conduct strike the upright critics of the day, trapped in their web of hierarchies, categories, and snobberies, and utterly incapable of following their Shepherd in drawing the full circle of human experience? After all, how could a rude, drinking fellow also be a genius, or how could a mere farmer actually presume to be an artist?

The artist tried to explain himself in his comic tale 'Dr David Dale's Account of a Grand Aerial Voyage'. This is a tall story about a poet named James Hogg who, along with the scientist and philosopher Dr Dale, flies away from Edinburgh under a gas balloon, 'on a voyage of discovery in the heavens'.[5] Luckily the two explorers are provided with six gallons of Glenlivat whiskey. They float through the clouds and up to the moon, the scientist engrossed in his calculations and the poet dancing, singing, and calling out to the stars:

The tempest may tout, and the wind may blaw
    With its whoo-rhoo, morning and even,
For now the auld Shepherd's aboon them a',
    Winging his way through the sternies of heaven.   stars
He has had dreams of the night an' the day,
    Journeys sublime by streamer and rainbow,   comet
Over the clifts of the milky-way,
    And by the light of the seraphim's window.

His 'journeys sublime' here of course represent Hogg's poems of
cosmic flight, such as 'Kilmeny' or *Pilgrims of the Sun*. As their
balloon returns to earth, the doctor, a man of gravity, announces,

> ' . . . . We have formed a great paracentrical parabola, and I
> think must come to the ground somewhere in the North
> Highlands. Do you know what a parabola is, James?'
> 'Ou, finely that, man. — Here's t'ye. — It is just a kind o'
> representation o' things by similitude — and a very good
> way it is. It answers poetry unco weel'.

The poet here is a little like Hamlet, a visionary who hints at the
truth while protecting himself behind a mask of folly. In these
lines we catch Hogg's defence of his art, his conception of poety in
contrast to science and philosophy, and his rather sad acceptance
of the dismissive response he received even from favourably-
disposed readers. The parabola 'answers poetry' uncommonly
well because it gives 'a kind o' representation o' things by
similitude', a useful metaphor for human desire and endeavour
within the larger context of apparently irresolvable opposites like
nature and spirit, subjective and objective, and individual and
social. A parabola is 'a very good way', a path leading to self-
knowledge, growth, and wholeness.

'Dr Dale's Account' ends with a new twist, a brief underwater
episode to contrast with the preceding aerial voyage. The balloon
splashes down in Loch Garry, but continues to drag onwards,
'whiles beneath the water and whiles above it; but always as the
Shepherd's head came above, he uttered a load Hilloa! in a half-
choked style'. The same innovative use of a contrasting journey at
the end occurs in another poem, 'A Dream', where the main
movement is down to a watery dreamworld as a mermaid leads the
poet

135

Far to her deep and crystal dome,
A radiant and pellucid home;
And there, upon a coral bed,
With oceans rolling o'er my head,
I lay in a delirious rest,
With beauty slumbering on my breast.
The swinging sun, far, far away,
Poured through the sea his silver ray,
And shed the softest shade of light —
'Twas neither noontide blaze nor night.
   No swelling surge nor floating foam
Approached that calm and peaceful home;
So soft the undulation played,
'Twas like an eve in twilight shade.[6]

'A Dream' is the exact mirror-image to 'Dr Dale's Account', with a mermaid (representing the unconscious) taking the place of the philosopher and scientist. Poet and guide wander hand-in-hand along the ocean floor, the poet marvelling at sights that embrace nature, humanity (— the bones of sailors —), and the supernatural, until the mermaid informs him that he is 'too gross for ocean maid'. In a lively finale she then takes him for a brief fling around the cosmos;

   But just as I began to dread
   Against a globe to break my head,
   Out through the curtains on the wall
   I bounced, and got a grievous fall —
   There lay astounded on the floor
   The wayward minstrel of the moor.

In other words, the downward journey into the unconscious, and the upward journey into imagination, both end in a return to earth and an acceptance of hard reality.

   His concept of a parabola also informs many of the satires written by Hogg in his last decade. Often these begin with savage indignation at the follies of others, then gradually the ridicule comes closer to home, and finally the satirist either laughs at his own failings or somehow affirms his kinship with a fallen human

race. 'Disagreeables; by the Ettrick Shepherd', starts by attacking
tailors, gluttons, and the pious spinsters of Edinburgh:

> AN OLD BLUE-STOCKING MAID! Oh! that's a being,
> That's hardly to be borne! Her saffron hue,
> Her thinnish lips, close primmed as they were sewn
> Up by a milliner, and made water-proof,
> To guard the fount of wisdom that's within.
> Her borrowed locks, of dry and withered hue,
> Her straggling beard of ill-conditioned hairs,
> And then her jaws of wise and formal cast;
> Chat-chat! chat-chat! Grand shrewd remarks! —
> That may have meaning — may have none for me.[7]

But when he avows his hatred of creditors, the satirist stumbles
upon the sobering truth:

> It is not the man,
> The friend who has obliged us, we would shun,
> But the conviction which his presence brings,
> That we have done him wrong.

There is more than a hint of Horace's influence in 'Disagreeables',
with its engaging description of contemporary types, its under-
stated contrasts, its urbane self-mockery and general skepticism,
and its movement from antagonism to implied self-knowledge and
community. Finally the satirist meets his double, his mirror-
image, in

> A BLUSTERING FELLOW! There's a deadly bore,
> Placed in a good man's way, who only yearns
> For happiness and joy. But day by day,
> This blusterer meets me, and the hope's defaced!
> I cannot say a word — make one remark,
> That meets not flat and absolute contradiction —

The blusterer is a kind of Gil-Martin, a figure who confronts the
narrator with a mirror-image of his own pride and alienation. As
in most of Hogg's satires, the narrator ends by laying aside his
satirical mask, to admit implicitly that he, too, has personal
failings.

137

K

A slight variation on this satiric formula is found in 'The Elder in Love'. At the start of this poem Hogg invites us to laugh at the churchman Gabriel, described by his kinsman Sir John as

> one so used to sit and grunt at church;
> To make wry faces, wink, and shake the head;
> Gather up halfpence in long-shafted ladles;
> . . .
> At funerals whine out long and stupid graces;
> And sing, 'O mother dear, Jerusalem!'
> In every saintly throng; a very slow-hound
> Upon the scent of sin.[8]

However by the end of the poem Gabriel has righted the balance by recounting his past suffering and his unfortunate love affair. In these satires the reader follows the poet's journey towards reconciliation and the perception of affinities. Similar works would include 'Dusty' (from the *Scottish Pastorals*), the *Confessions*, 'The First Sermon', and other semi-satirical stories like the excellent 'Sound Morality' or 'On the Separate Existence of the Soul'. 'Scenes of Other Worlds', which Hogg courageously published in Belfast, finds a satirical balance between the (Protestant) King William and the (Catholic) King James, with both monarchs ending up, according to the Shepherd, 'In that dim and desolate globe, assigned by the mighty Ruler of the universe to the shades of departed warriors for a residence, until the crimes done in their days of nature are thoroughly washed away, and repented of'.[9]

Hogg also brought out several literary parodies in his last years. In his 'Andrew the Packman: After the manner of Wordsworth', a garrulous poetic Englishman harangues a poor pedlar on the need for religious orthodoxy. As he rattles on, the boring 'Wordsworth' observes with satisfaction that his listener is gradually 'overcome':

> He look'd three ways at once, then other three,
> Which did make six; and three, and three, and three,
> (Which, as I reckon, made fifteen in all,)
> So many ways did that o'er-master'd pedlar
> Look in one moment's space. Then did he give
> Three hems most audible, which, to mine ear

As plainly said as English tongue could say,
'I'm conquer'd! I'm defeated! And I yield,
And bow before the majesty of Truth!'
   He went away — he gave his pack one hitch
Up on his stooping shoulders; then with gait
Of peddling uniformity, and ell
In both his hands held firm across that part
Of man's elongated and stately form
In horses call'd the rump, he trudged him on,
Whistling a measure most iniquitous.
I was amaz'd; yet could not choose but smile
At this defeated pedlar's consecution;
And thus said to myself, my left cheek still
Leaning upon my palm . . . . [10]

These devastating lines take on a new interest if we recall the Edinburgh rumour that the Pedlar in Wordsworth's poem *The Excursion* was based on the character of the Ettrick Shepherd.[11] Wordworth's poetry seemed to Hogg to be dangerously imbued with personal absolutism, stagnation, and a reductive fixation on the natural, physical aspects of life. For Hogg the journey into the physical was incomplete unless it brought an awareness of the potential horror of that lower world, and a determination to escape it. Nature is beautiful, and cannot be denied, but it is also deceptive, it retains always a tremendous capacity for chaos and suffering. The important thing in Hogg's vision is movement; a mature person accepts nature, in himself and the world, yet also tries to transcend that ever-present reality by carrying its truths back to a social world.

The same turn of thought accounts for the Shepherd's suspicion of modernising trends in politics, which he consistently feared as a surrender to an urban chaos ruled by competitive economics,

> the throne abused,
> And rank confusion worse confused;
> All peace and order set to jar —
> In every corner roaring war;
> . . .
> To sponge and grub for sordid pelf,
> Nothing in view but self! self! self![12]

Hogg's comic tale 'On the Separate Existence of the Soul' attacks liberal economic theory through the figure of a rich, progressive young laird, who tries to run his country estate by introducing modern improvements and quoting from Adam Smith; the laird is humiliated and made to change places with his shepherd, a simple man who 'steadily upheld the propriety of keeping by old-established customs, and of improving these leisurely and prudently'.[13] In Hogg's view capitalism seemed likely to destroy community and bring in a new tyranny of uniformity and mercenary motives. When he sees, then, the new type of schoolteacher,

> the modern prig,
> With well-starch'd collar, hair of formal cut,
> Thin listless clasp and independent strut,
> I weep to think that the great magic fountain
> Of Scotland's glory and ascendency
> Is soil'd with lucre, mudded in the spring.[14]

Another social satire is Hogg's 'The Last Stork'. The graceful giant storks make yearly journeys from the Nile, Jordan, and other Mediterranean areas, to Britain, bringing with them (as poets do) associations with history, religion, and nature. The people of England have started shooting the storks and selling them for meat, however, and now only one of these birds (apparently representing Hogg himself) flies to Britain, where a 'sporting Bishop'[15] cheerfully shoots him for dinner. The 'fair journeyer of the sky' delivers a long dying speech predicting ruin as the result of Britain's 'base venality'.

Politically the Shepherd was a moderate and traditionalist, equally opposed to radical innovation, on one side, and to the new 'aristocracy' of farming'[16] on the other. Both the Whig and Tory policies of the day, he maintained, were destroying community spirit by making 'the distance between master and servant wider and wider', until by 1832

> The menial of course feels that he is no more a member of a community, but a slave; a servant of servants, a mere tool of labour in the hand of a man whom he knows or deems inferior to himself, and the joy of his spirit is mildewed. He is

140

a moping, sullen, melancholy man, flitting from one master to another in hopes to find heart's ease and contentment, — but he finds it not.

In the early 1790's 'every farmer had only one farm', but by the 1830's 'every farmer has three, four, or ten of these farms'. The inevitable result was 'such a distance between servants and masters, that in fact they have no communication whatever, and very little interest in common'. Farm workers had gained better food and housing, but to Hogg's mind they were simultaneously being reduced to 'a state of absolute slavery, with only one amelioration, namely, the liberty, at each term, of selling themselves to the highest bidder'. This made a sad contrast with the time of Hogg's youth, when 'every master sat at the head of his kitchen table, and shared the meal with his servants', when every farmhouse 'formed a little community of its own, of which each member was conscious of bearing an important part'. 'In my young days', the old Shepherd adds, 'we had singing matches almost every night', together with dances, kirns and harvest suppers, and whole days set aside for fairs, weddings, and athletic contests such as 'wrestling, leaping, racing on foot, putting the stone, archery, and numberless others'. There had been, apparently, a sense of 'family union, or compact', a togetherness of old and young, female and male, and masters and workers.

One other cause of decaying community was the influence of gamekeepers, those 'most vexatious, insolent, and insignificant persons in the whole world'. Hogg implies that gamekeepers were often secretly in league with professional poachers, and for this very reason 'If a gentleman chance to transgress by going over his bounds; or, if a farmer's friend or servant is found in transgression, . . . then they are amazingly active and efficient indeed, and the humble culprit is soused with the utmost rigour of law'. It seems that the local aristocrats had much to answer for; Hogg names his own landlord, the young Duke of Buccleuch, whom he blames for his choice of gamekeeper, as well as for hiring 'companies of Englishmen'[17] who annually scoured the countryside to exterminate 'the mole, that innocent and blessed little pioneer who enriches our pastures'. Moles were beneficial to farming, Hogg thought, and the systematic slaughter of moles was 'the most unnatural of all persecutions that ever was raised'; on

141

principle he opposed 'the system of extermination with regard to any class of creatures with which the all-wise Creator of the universe has seen meet to stock a country'. 'The change that has taken place in our country in the course of the last thirty years', he concludes,

> is truly melancholy to an old fellow like me. Our beautiful every-green gairs, which were literally covered with mole-hills every summer, on which the ewes lay and the lambs sported, and on which the grass was as dark green and as fine and finer than any of the daisied fields of Lothian, alas! where are they now? All vanished and become the coarsest of the soil, and thus the most beautiful feature of the pastoral country is annihilated.

Until his early sixties James Hogg remained 'a strongly-built, active, muscular man', 'a lover of out-of-doors amusement, of athletic exercises, running, wrestling, and leaping, — an angler by the stream, and a hunter on the hills'.[18] He was the captain of an archery club and helped each year to organise the St Ronan's Border Games, where he 'exerted himself lustily' in various sporting events, seldom neglecting 'to carry off some of the prizes, to the astonishment of his vanquished juniors'.[19] On one bright October Friday, Hogg 'won cleverly' an archery contest at Innerleithen, and then presided as croupier for an evening of 'the greatest glee' at Riddle's Inn. The next morning

> eight of the most celebrated fishers of which the banks of the Tweed can boast, started for a day's salmon-fishing for a considerable bet; and upon weighing the fish caught by the various competitors, the glory of the day was declared in favour of the Ettrick Shepherd. It is but justice to state, that Mr Hogg had only a small trouting rod, and without a reel, and that one of his salmon weighed twenty pounds, three ounces, and a half, and was the largest fish caught in the country this season with the rod.[20]

A friend recalls Hogg returning home one day with 'a heavy creel of trouts', treating his guests to 'broth of the best, trout, lamb and haggis', and speaking with pride of the upcoming

Border Games, 'where wrestling, pitching the bar, throwing the sledge-hammer, and archery, are practiced . . . , and in which the Shepherd himself takes a leading part'; after showing his library ('a small but valuable collection'), the poet brought out his 'good yew bow six feet long', before settling down to mix toddy in 'a massive punch-bowl'.[21] At the Candlemaker Row Festival, an annual gathering held in his honour by Edinburgh's apprentices, Hogg would lead the way in a New Year's celebration of dining, drinking, singing, and curling. 'I had very nigh won the gold medal and lost it three times almost by a hairs breadth', he wrote to his wife, adding that he 'gained great honour as a player and presided at the festival'[22] — to which Margaret replied, twelve days later, 'What in the world has become of you, you promised to be home a week ago . . . all I shall say is if you are well it is too bad & beg you to come home'.[23]

Even the old teacher, so hated by James Hogg a half-century earlier, was now a valued friend. In a cancelled passage from 'The Dominie', Hogg pictured himself meeting the teacher 'weekly or so'[24] to seek his 'profound advice', or simply to go together

> To the snug country alehouse. How his heart
> Would lighten up and he would talk of Homer
> Of Eschylus and even of Zoroaster
> In language most intense and dignified
> Burns he liked not! On hearing him extolled
> He shook his head and bade me rather take
> Isaiah for a model or adopt
> The stile of one John Milton. Then his eye
> His old grey eye would gleam, and he would clap
> His hand upon his knee with loud ha-ha
> And say 'Daft poet! Foolish poet! Ah what notions
> Revel in your crazed head! Give me your hand
> I must confess my old heart warms to you
> For all your fictions and extravagance'.

In 1829 Hogg was caught poaching on the Duke of Buccleuch's land. His nine-year lease on Mount Benger was up for renewal at the time, and it is not surprising that the Duke chose to evict him and demand the rent that was owing. James and Margaret were ruined, losing most of their possessions in a forced auction, selling their sheep at a loss, and moving back into the four-room cottage at Altrive. Here they crowded together with their four children (a fifth would arrive shortly) and their new lodger Mr Brooks, 'a gentleman of weak mind'.[25] They still continued to receive lengthy visits from relatives, sportsmen, literary worthies, aspiring poets, and 'English students, mounted on grand horses', who 'think themselves exceedingly great men'.[26]

James Hogg had his revenge against the Duke's gamekeeper by writing a child's story called 'The Poachers'. The hero is a boy, Benjy, whose starving parents are driven to hunt rabbits on property that belongs to the baronet Sir John. Benjy's father is arrested, all their goods are sold by auction, and his mother dies of grief. The father later returns to poaching, and is shot and killed by the gamekeeper. Knowing that Cocket, Benjy's dog, has learned the art of poaching, the evil gamekeeper tries

> to hang up the little animal before his master's eyes. Benjy darted off like an arrow, and Cocket before him. They were pursued, and would soon have been overtaken, but Benjy had a protector for Cocket in view; and, presenting Johnnie Cope, who was loaded with swan-shot, he cocked, and then said to his assailants, 'Now touch outher me or my dog gin ye daur for the blood o' ye! I shall lay your heads where ye never shall lift them again. My dog is a treasure left me by my poor father, an' ye hae nae mair right to take him frae me than I hae to come an' take Sir John's house an' garden frae him'.[27]

Benjy runs away, finds a home for himself and Cocket, studies very hard at school, and years later he marries Sir John's daughter.

There were many trips to Edinburgh for the Shepherd in these last years. It was his practice to lodge 'a week or a fortnight' in Candlemaker Row. Here the early hours would often find him in 'some fifth storey in the Old Town, where a young tradesman of literary tastes had collected six or eight lads' eager to hear the man of genius sing 'many of his own songs' and tell his 'droll stories'.[28]

On one of these visits Hogg decided to sail down to London, where he arrived on the first of January 1832. With his 'eyes puckered up by wrinkles, his cheek and lips, and teeth, expressing the most natural laughter',[29] he soon became a public favourite, invited to clubs and dinner-parties, flattered by famous or wealthy admirers, and made the guest of honour at a Burns' Night Banquet. The scandalised Dr Browne records that in London — that 'great Babel of the South' — Hogg was 'raised far above his proper sphere', and had the audacity to set about 'singing songs in praise of all . . . things that have earned a pre-eminent title to the detestation of mankind'.[30] Nevertheless, during his three months in London Hogg was apparently offered a knighthood (which he turned down), and found a publisher willing to bring out a collected edition of his stories.

Back in Scotland in April, Hogg imagined he had solved his financial worries. Unfortunately his new publisher went bankrupt before the end of the month. His *Altrive Tales* (— a slightly belligerent title —) died after only one volume.

Whatever their circumstances, James and Margaret knew how to be happy. In their garden they planted sweet peas, lupins, mignonettes and other flowers, onions, carrots and turnips, peas and beans, parsley, lettuce, cress, radishes, and leeks.[31] 'I never knew either man or woman who has been so uniformly happy as I have been',[32] James could boast, while in a poem to his wife he asked,

> O wha are sae happy as me an' my Moggy?
> O wha are sae happy as Moggy an' me?
> We're baith turnin' auld, an' our walth is soon tauld,
> But contentment bides aye in our cottage sae wee.
> . . . .
> Our duke may hae goud mair than schoolmen can reckon   gold
> And flunkies to watch ilka glance o' his ee,   every; eye
> His lady aye braw sittin prim in the ha';   so fine
> But are they sae happy as Moggy an' me?[33]

Robert Gillies explains, 'I believe he had no great respect (perhaps none at all) for the judgment of our wise world, and thought the best practical rule for a shepherd poet was to keep on his way rejoicing, as long as he could, regardless of praise or blame'.[34] But in some works Hogg expresses great frustration at his isolation as an artist and thinker. His isolation has both a poetic and religious dimension in 'The Summer Midnight', when

145

he discusses his loneliness, his difficulty in finding an appropriate audience, and his approaching death:

> O for some sadly dying note
> Upon this silent hour to float,
> Where, from the headlong world remote,
>   The lyre might wake its melody.[35]

In his final years, James Hogg wrote a great many songs, poems, tales, and satires, as well as books on Sir Walter Scott and Robert Burns, and his volume of *Lay Sermons*. His song 'Love Came to the Door o' My Heart' recalls an earlier time when he was 'filled . . . with wild dismay' after Cupid had knocked at his door. 'Gae away, gae away, thou wicked wean', he had cried; but eventually he had learned to accept Love and to leave the door of his heart ajar:

> And what do you think? — by day and by night,
>   For these ten long years and twain,
> I have cherish'd the urchin with fondest delight,
>   And we'll never mair part again.[36]

Some of his finest stories, including 'The Unearthly Witness', 'Strange Letter of a Lunatic', 'The Barber of Duncow', and 'The Watchmaker', appeared in the Shepherd's last four years. Perhaps the most telling of these is 'Scottish Haymakers', a short piece which revives several aspects of the *Confessions*, and begins where Robert Wringhim ended, at the side of a hay-wagon. Three poets (Hogg, Scott, and Grieve) are out walking with two actors and two painters, Peter and Alexander Naesmith. The seven artists meet a group of haymakers, and Monsieur Alexandre, one of the actors, uses ventriloquism to make the labourers think that a baby is being smothered under the hay, or else that their wagon is haunted. It seems the artists are oblivious to the extra work they create for the poor labourers, who frantically unload their hay searching for a child while the men of supposedly high sensibilities stand and watch. At length, 'Mr Scott and I', Hogg writes, 'stripped off our coats, and assisted',[37] yet still their friends enjoy laughing smugly at the expense of the peasants. The artists then proceed to a nearby tavern, where Monsieur Alexandre in effect assumes Gil-Martin's role by seeming to raise demons:

> Then there was a drunken man came to the door, and insisted in a rough obstreperous manner on being let in to shoot Mr Hogg; on which the landlord ran to the door and bolted it . . . . We all heard the voice of the man going round and round the house, grumbling, swearing, and threatening, and all the while Alexandre was just standing with his back to us at the room-door, always holding his hand to his mouth . . . . At length, on calling [the barmaid] in to serve us with some wine and toddy, we heard the drunken man's voice coming in at the top of the chimney. Such a state of amazement as Jane was in I never beheld. 'But ye neednae be feared, gentlemen,' said she, 'for I'll defy him to win down. The door's boltit an' lockit, an' the vent o' the lumb is na sae wide as that jug'.
>
> However, down he came, and down he came, until his voice actually seemed to be coming out of the grate. Jane ran for it, saying, 'He is winning down, I believe, after a'. He is surely the deil!'

This is clearly reminiscent of certain scenes near the ends of *both* narratives in the *Confessions*, and it seems, therefore, that Hogg is using 'Scottish Haymakers' as a commentary on his greatest novel.

The theme of 'Scottish Haymakers' is the relationship between life and art. Hogg has taken an event from his own past, reduced it to its simple, most universal aspects, and given it a balanced structure to emphasise the need for human fellowship. The tale balances seven artists against seven labourers, with the author himself, despite being officially cast as one of the artists, showing obvious signs of divided loyalty. Another neat division is between the two equal halves of the story, the first half ending when one of the haymakers 'ran off, and never once looked over his shoulder', living afterwards 'in a deranged state of mind', and the second half ending with one of the artists leaving the inn, running, falling, and receiving an injury that 'ultimately occasioned his death'. The trivial art of Monsieur Alexandre is a betrayal of the common people, whereas the story as a whole has the opposite effect, reminding us through thoughtful, evocative parallels that the artist and the worker are both human beings, united by their nearness to chaos and subjection to the unreliable, often hostile, forces of nature.

'It is amazing how little makes a good picture', says the painter Alexander Naesmith to James Hogg; 'and frequently the less that is taken in the better'. The words are Hogg's challenge to readers to find the hard-won simplicity and clarity of his 'Scottish Haymakers', and also, by implication, of his *Confessions*. But regrettably most readers and critics have been more like the workers of 'Scottish Haymakers', duped by the illusion, the spectacle, and failing to see the more central aspects of symbol, design, purpose, and theme.

'I dislike all fine and splendid writing', Hogg states in his *Lay Sermons*, 'and admire plain common sense much more'. He thought most of the popular fiction of his time 'nothing but froth and fume' because it gave 'a transient and false view of human life; the figures are overcharged with colouring, the whole is intended to please, and there is nothing in the background to teach us that all is vanity'.

For more than a century-and-a-half the Ettrick Shepherd has been so often absurdly misrepresented as being reactionary, resentful, foolish, naive, or uneducated, that it is only fair to give a few excerpts from his little-known book of *Lay Sermons*, the one work in which he addresses readers most directly and sincerely. In it Hogg defends the 'great principles of universal equity which are common to states and individuals, and by which the rights of both ought to be adjusted'. He argues in favour of 'liberal arts' and 'the cultivation of universal love and peace', and devotes a whole chapter to discussing the 'enormous wickedness' of

> the art of war, . . . the most dangerous of any. It leads to no aim or end besides the taking of life. . . . Every victory is a new starting place from which to unleash the dogs of havoc.

Many famous writers were in Hogg's view guilty of glorifying warfare and the 'criminal' deeds of military leaders so that they would be 'lauded by gaping crowds of slavish and stupid people'. The Shepherd concludes that 'all men of wit and learning' should 'unite their endeavours and talents to bring the system of destruction into discredit, that the sword may not devour for ever'. In a later chapter Hogg asserts that 'we are all flowers of the Almighty's garden, and though of different hues, shall all bloom together with him in Paradise'.

The *Lay Sermons* express great scorn for formal education. According to Hogg, girls were being 'compelled to attend to a course of flimsy studies which serves to dissipate their minds', with the result that 'we find so many beautiful and agreeable women more ignorant than they should be'. As for the education given to boys at that time, Hogg simply avers his 'utter contempt' for 'the whole parade of college education'; 'I have listened to many lectures of the most able professors', he explains, 'and it is perfectly obvious to me that they are of no avail whatever to the students, but just go in the one ear and out at the other'. Yet on the other hand Hogg urges his readers never to 'cease at any period of life to increase your knowledge, and, by exercise, to improve the powers of your understanding':

> I therefore conceive that the best species of discipline . . . is to subject our minds . . . to vigorous exercises as long as we are able; for I am certain that exercise and temperance preserve the body in a sound state; and equally certain, that delightful study, the exercise of the mind, gives full vigour to its powers until extreme old age.

Hogg was unable to agree with the notion that 'there is a given period' in any person's life 'at which he should retire' from mental exertion and from reading: 'I earnestly recommend it', he tells us, 'never to allow your minds to sink below the tone and vigour which mark their natural strength'. Hogg's own reading at this time (according to the evidence in his *Lay Sermons*) included Shakespeare, Swift, Voltaire, Pope, Scott, Wordsworth, *Tristram Shandy*, 'Ladies' novels', 'translations . . . of the ancients' (especially Homer), Burns, Byron, the American Washington Irving, and the Swiss poet Lavater.

Only in the *Lay Sermons* does Hogg discuss explicitly and at length his central unifying symbol of the journey. Creative writing, he says, is a 'mental journey' requiring 'original powers of mind' and 'the fire and rapidity of true genius' in order to break free of 'chains and fetters' and 'overstep the cold restraints of [formal] art':

> Genius may be defined as taste put in motion and dis-
> played: and I firmly believe, when a man is animated by the
> fire of nature, and his mind brought to its full tone of exer-
> tion, that he will write more consistently with . . . common
> sense, than if fettered with the best rules.

Reading, too, should resemble a journey. A novel or poem should be able 'to rouse and carry [us] along, with an irresistable force', so that we appreciate its shape, direction, and sense of imaginative freedom and movement:

> If the author carries you into the regions of fancy, and
> amuses you with a creation of new and beautiful images,
> why not approve of them, though of a different political
> creed? If he goes along the beaten road of nature, and intro-
> duces you to characters . . . such as you meet with in the
> world, why not converse with him as you do with a friend?
> You ought to give yourself no trouble . . . provided he takes
> you along with him, and makes an agreeable companion on
> the road.

> I adjure you all, then, my young friends, that when you find
> the inspiration and power of the author carrying you along
> with him, take a polite leave of the reviewers in as easy a
> manner as you can. You have learned the mystery of the art .
> . . to a much greater advantage than ever you will learn it
> from them.

Far from reading in a merely passive, unquestioning manner, we should try to share the author's sense of journey, excitement, and discovery, while at the same time entering into a kind of dialogue or debate with the author: 'Sit down to your book as you would to conversation', Hogg advises:

> I would prefer that exercise of the understanding, which . . .
> makes us master of the thoughts of the author, which en-
> ables us to relish them, and to see their full force and beauty

as we go along. This exercise of the understanding is of great value. It is acquired by attention to what you read, much more than by reading a great deal.

The *Lay Sermons* exhort us to read 'with precision and force' and to look for themes, irony, and purpose:

> I never yet knew a young lady the better of her reading when she read for excitement alone. Never expect to be deceived into wisdom, nor to find it when you are not in search of it. The road lies through thickets of briers and thorns, and there are some steep ascents by the way of so hazardous a nature, that you require some resolution to carry you forward. But if you come immediately into meadows of flowers . . . you have reason to fear that you have mistaken the road.

At sixty-three, James Hogg felt that he was near the end of his 'long journey through life' when he wrote his *Lay Sermons*. It had been a 'Perilous voyage', he declares:

> Take a prospect of human life through the vista of reason, and you must perceive that it is a voyage to an undiscovered country. Our provisions wear out, and the vessel turns crazy as we advance. It is a voyage which we have begun, and which we should try to bring to as happy and prosperous a termination as possible. What, then, can we do better than to lay in a good store of provisions, to have honest and true messmates, and with all our skill to steer clear of the quick-sands which would swallow us up, and the rocks on which we may be dashed to pieces. With these precautions . . . we shall enter the harbour with hope, and look back on the dangers that we have escaped with pleasure and exultation.

The Ettrick Shepherd got his first glimpse of this final harbour when a physician told him that he had 'water in the chest'. For a few years after the diagnosis Hogg 'seemed to laugh at the idea, and pronounced it impossible, as one drop of water he never drank'. His health declined rapidly in September 1835, although in October he was well enough to spend 'a few days . . . angling in the Tweed'. On the third day of this fishing trip, Hogg walked back to Cameron's Hotel in Innerleithen for a game of billiards with an old friend:

> but no sooner had we commenced the game, than poor Hogg was seized with a most violent trembling. A glass of brandy was instantly got, and swallowed; still the trembling continued, and a second was got, which produced the desired effect. At this moment the Yarrow carrier was passing the inn, on his way to Edinburgh, when Mr. Hogg called him in, and desired him to sit down until he would draw an order on the Commercial Bank for twenty pounds. . . . After various attempts he found it impossible even to sign his name, and was, therefore, obliged to tell the carrier that he must of necessity defer drawing the order until next week. The carrier, however, took out his pocket-book, and handed the Shepherd a five-pound note

as a loan. Hogg was now feeling the first effects of paralysis. He immediately called a carriage and returned to Altrive. It soon became clear he was dying 'of what the country folks call black jaundice'.[38]

James Hogg died on November 21st, 1835, at the age of sixty-four. One of his last poems (— a revised version of some lines from *Queen Hynde* —) is addressed to his women readers, and makes the best possible summary of the literary life of the Ettrick Shepherd:

> Maid of my worship thou shalt see
> Though long I strove to pleasure thee
> That now I've changed my timid tone
> And sing to please myself alone
> And thou wilt read when well I wot
> I care not whether you do or not
>   Yes I'll be querulous or boon
> Flow with the tide change with the moon
> For what am I or what art thou
> Or what the cloud and radiant bow
> Or what are waters winds and seas
> But elemental energies?
> The sea must flow the cloud descend
> The thunder burst the rainbow bend

Not when they would, but when they can
Fit emblems of the soul of man!
Then let me frolic while I may
The sportive vagrant of a day
Yield to the impulse of the time
Be it a toy or shrine sublime
Wing the thin air or starry sheen
Sport with the child upon the green
Dive to the sea-maid's coral dome
Or fairy's visionary home
Sail on the whirlwind or the storm
Or trifle with the maiden's form
Or raise up spirits of the hill
But only if and when I will
　　Say may the meteor of the wild
Nature's unstaid erratic child
That glimmers o'er the forest fen
Or twinkles in the darksome glen
Cat that be bound? Can that be rein'd
By cold ungenial rules restrained?
No! leave it o'er its ample home
The boundless wilderness to roam
To gleam to tremble and to die
'Tis Nature's error — so am I
Then leave to all his fancies wild
Nature's own rude untutored child
And should he forfeit his fond claim
Pity his loss — but do not blame
　　Let those who list the garden choose
Where flowers are regular and profuse
Come thou to dell and lonely lea
And cull the mountain gems with me
And sweeter blooms may be thine own
By nature's hand at random sown
And sweeter strains may touch thy heart
Than are producible by art
The nightingale may give delight
A while 'mid silence of the night
But the lark lost in the heavens blue
O her wild strain is ever new![39]

153

Notes

1 Dr Robert Macnish, *The Modern Pythagorean* (Edinburgh, 1838), quoted in Karl Miller, *Cockburn's Millenium* (London, 1975), p. 207.
2 Anon. revs. in *British Critic*, July 1824, pp. 68-69; *Westminster Review*, Apr. 1825, p. 531; *Examiner*, 1 Aug. 1824, p. 483; *Emmet*, 18 Oct. 1823, p. 26; and *Ayr Correspondent*, 31 Dec. 1824, p. 30
3 *Memoirs, Journal and Correspondence of Thomas Moore*, 8 vols., ed. Russell (London, 1854), V. 12.
4 Julian Charles Young, *Journal* (London, 1871), quoted in A. L. Strout, *Life and Letters of James Hogg*, pp. 268-69.
5 'Dr David Dale's Account of a Grand Aerial Voyage', *Edinburgh Literary Journal*, 23 Jan. 1830, pp. 50-54.
6 Hogg, 'A Dream', *Fraser's Magazine*, May 1835, pp. 516-17.
7 Hogg, 'Disagreeables', *Fraser's Magazine*, June 1831, pp. 567-69.
8 Hogg, 'The Elder in Love', *Fraser's Magazine*, Mar. 1832, pp. 234-37.
9 Hogg, 'Scenes of Other Worlds', *Belfast Magazine*, Feb. 1825, pp. 49-56.
10 Hogg, 'Andrew the Packman', *Edinburgh Literary Journal*, 20 Mar. 1830, pp. 179-80.
11 See (Lockhart), *Peter's Letters*, I, 140-42.
12 Hogg, 'The Magic Mirror', *Blackwood's Magazine*, Oct. 1831, pp. 650-54.
13 Hogg, 'On the Separate Existence of the Soul', rpt. in *James Hogg: Selected Stories and Sketches*, ed. Douglas S. Mack, pp. 180-95.
14 Hogg, 'The Dominie', *Edinburgh Literary Journal*, 26 Mar. 1831, p. 199.
15 Hogg, 'The Last Stork', in his *A Queer Book* (Edinburgh and London, 1832), pp. 300-16.
16 Hogg, 'On the Changes in the Habits, Amusements, and Conditions of the Scottish Peasantry', *Quarterly Journal of Agriculture*, Sept. 1832, pp. 256-63.
17 'Mr Hogg on the Effects of Mole-Catching', *Quarterly Journal of Agriculture*, Aug. 1829, pp. 640-45.
18 Anon., 'The Life and Literary Progress of James Hogg, the Ettrick Shepherd', *Edinburgh Literary Gazette*, 27 June 1829, p. 97.
19 Lockhart, *Life of Sir Walter Scott, Bart.*, V, 317.
20 Anon., 'St Ronan's Bowmen', *Edinburgh Weekly Journal*, 3 Nov. 1830, p. 349.
21 C., 'Abbotsford', *Atheneum*, 13 Aug. 1831, p. 520.
22 James Hogg, letter to Margaret, 1 Jan. 1831, printed in Parr, *James Hogg at Home*, p. 85.
23 Margaret Hogg, letter to James, 12 Jan. 1831, printed in Parr, *James Hogg at Home*, p. 85.
24 From Hogg's untitled draft, MS. Papers 42, Item 54, Alexander Turnbull Library.

25 Mary Garden, *Memorials of James Hogg, the Ettrick Shepherd* (London, 1885), p. 313n.
26 Hogg, 'A Very Ridiculous Sermon', *Fraser's Magazine*, Feb. 1835, pp. 226-31.
27 Hogg, 'The Poachers', *Ackermann's Juvenile Forget-me-Not* (1831), pp. 99-116.
28 *Select Writings of Robert Chambers*, 7 vols. (Edinburgh, 1847), II, 23, 24.
29 Anon., 'Fine Arts', *Gentleman's Magazine*, May 1832, p. 349.
30 *'Life' of the Ettrick Shepherd Anatomized*, p. 4.
31 See Parr, *James Hogg at Home*, pp. 76-77.
32 Hogg, 'Memoir', p. 54.
33 In 'The Shepherd's Noctes, and the Reason Why They Do Not Appear in Fraser's Magazine', *Fraser's Magazine*, July 1833, p. 51.
34 Gillies, *Memoirs*, II, 242.
35 Hogg, 'The Summer Midnight', *Sheffield Iris*, 26 July 1831, n.p.
36 Hogg, 'Love Came to the Door o' My Heart', *McLeod's Original Scottish Melodies* (Edinburgh, c. 1835), pp. 17-20.
37 Hogg, 'Scottish Haymakers', *Forget Me Not* (1834), pp. 326-35. Reprinted in *James Hogg: Tales of Love and Mystery*.
38 P. Boyd, cited in William Howitt, *The Homes and Haunts of the British Poets* (1847; rpt. London, 1862), pp. 389-90.
39 In Hogg's letter to Mr S. C. Hall, c. 1835. Printed by permission of the Yale University Library.

CONCLUSION

IF James Hogg was betrayed by the critics of his day, his reputation received the kiss of death from Victorian editors who brought out so-called 'collected' editions of his poetry and prose. These massive, bowdlerised volumes, still unfortunately common in libraries, have encouraged a drastic underestimation of Hogg's genius.

He did, of course, write some mediocre poems, either in his early years or while trying to pay the rent at Mount Benger. It is these melodramatic or sentimental pieces which the poetry editors of 1838, 1852, and 1865 preserved with wearying devotion, while simply excluding fifty or more of Hogg's better short poems without mention, giving lobotomised versions of *The Queen's Wake* or *Mador of the Moor*, and turning lively songs into third-rate poems by printing them without music. Also excluded from these editions were most of his social satires, nearly half of his literary parodies, his poems addressed to Byron and Burns, and almost anything that might have seemed controversial. Anyone who tries to read these collections is likely to conclude that James Hogg was a respectable, harmless (in other words, brainless) innocent.

Equally horrible editions of Hogg's prose appeared in 1837, 1865, and 1884. The Shepherd was 'improved' by being placed in a Victorian straight-jacket of unimaginative respectability which ensured that he would be virtually forgotten during most of the twentieth century. Again the best pieces were left out, from the 'Love Adventures of Mr George Cochrane' to 'Dr David Dale's Account', 'Strange Letter of a Lunatic', 'The Barber of Duncow', 'Seeking the Houdy', and 'Scottish Haymakers'.

Critics during the century-and-a-quarter after Hogg's death did little to overcome the barriers erected by Hogg's victorious editors. Useful work by George Douglas or A. L. Strout was often overshadowed by supercilious, bemused commentators who mainly wanted to laugh at the Shepherd's peasant origins, rural manners, or national culture. Even the author of *Father and Son* saw the *Confessions* as little more than 'frenzied narrative',[1] while at the opposite extreme a sympathetic critic could be equally limiting in imputing to Hogg 'a dreamy sort of imagination, prolific, but not under control'.[2]

Hogg's *Confessions* has begun to attract the attention it deserves, thanks to perceptive editions by T. E. Welby (1924), André Gide (1947), and John Carey (1969). Some of the best criticism is contained in the Introductions to these volumes, as well as in the recent Introductions to *Brownie of Bodsbeck*, *Three Perils of Man*, *Memoir of the Author's Life and Familiar Anecdotes of Sir Walter Scott*, *Selected Stories and Sketches*, and *Anecdotes of Sir W. Scott*. Still, however, a number of central works are only available either in rare first editions or in subsequent mutilated texts: these would include the *Scottish Pastorals*, *Spy*, *Queen's Wake*, *Mador of the Moor*, *Three Perils of Woman*, and *Lay Sermons*.

Despite the efforts of grave-robbing, ring-snatching critics, the past two decades have seen the beginnings of a revival for James Hogg. His *Confessions* is available in several recent editions, and is taught on university courses around the world. The James Hogg Society now holds annual meetings, and publishes an annual *Newsletter* through Stirling University.

Hogg never called attention to the precision, clarity, and deep resonance of his best art. There is an appropriate irony in the fact that the self-proclaimed 'poet' in *The Three Perils of Man* cannot understand the meaning of the journey, while the *true* artist of that story turns out to be the simple, robust Charlie Scott. And in *The Queen's Wake* the apparently inferior harp is actually the best and most lasting. The essential writings of James Hogg always improve on a second and third reading, since they challenge us to see beneath the obvious surface of plot, spectacle, and direct statement, to find symbolism, ironies, and aesthetic shape.

Notes

1   Edmund Gosse, *Silhouettes* (London, 1925), p. 125.
2   Henry Thew Stephenson, *The Ettrick Shepherd: A Biography* (Bloomington, Indiana, 1922), p. 93,

SELECTED BIBLIOGRAPHY

I Books by James Hogg

There is no complete bibliography of works by James Hogg. A more extensive listing may be found in Edith Batho's *The Ettrick Shepherd* (Cambridge, 1927).

Scottish Pastorals (Edinburgh: Taylor, 1801).

The Mountain Bard (Edinburgh: Constable, and London: Murray, 1807).

The Shepherd's Guide (Edinburgh: Constable, and London: Murray, 1807).

The Forest Minstrel (Edinburgh and London: Constable, 1810).

The Spy: A Periodical Paper, of Literary Amusement and Instruction (Edinburgh: Robertson, 1810, and Aikman, 1810-1811.

The Queen's Wake (Edinburgh: Goldie, and London: Longman, 1813.)

The Hunting of Badlewe: A Dramatic Tale (London: Colborne, and Edinburgh: Goldie, 1814).

The Pilgrims of the Sun (London: Murray, and Edinburgh: Blackwood, 1815).

The Poetic Mirror; or The Living Bards of Britain (London: Longman, and Edinburgh: Ballantyne, 1816).

Mador of the Moor (Edinburgh: Blackwood, and London: Murray, 1816).

Dramatic Tales, 2 vols. (Edinburgh: Ballantyne, and London: Longman, 1817).

The Brownie of Bodsbeck; and Other Tales, 2 vols. (Edinburgh: Blackwood, and London: Murray, 1818).

The Long Pack; A Northumbrian Tale, An Hundred Years Old (Newcastle: Quay, 1818).

No. 1 of the Border Garland (Edinburgh: Gow, 1819).

The Jacobite Relics of Scotland, 2 vols, (Edinburgh: Blackwood, and London: Cadell, 1819, 1821).

Winter Evening Tales, collected among the Cottagers of the South of Scotland, 2 vols. (Edinburgh: Oliver and Boyd, and London: Whittaker, 1820).

The Poetical Works of James Hogg, 4 vols. (Edinburgh: Constable, and London: Hurst, Robinson, 1822).

The Royal Jubilee: A Scottish Mask (Edinburgh: Blackwood, and London: Cadell, 1822).

The Three Perils of Man; or, War, Women, and Witchcraft, 3 vols. (London: Longman, 1822).

The Three Perils of Woman; or, Love, Leasing, and Jealousy, 3 vols. (London: Longman, 1823).

The Private Memoirs and Confessions of a Justified Sinner; Written by Himself: with a detail of curious traditionary facts & other evidence by the editor (London: Longman, 1824).

Queen Hynde: A Poem, in six books (London: Longman, and Edinburgh: Blackwood, 1824).

Select and Rare Scottish Melodies: The Poetry by the Celebrated Ettrick Shepherd, The Symphonies and Accompaniments Composed . . . By Henry R. Bishop (London: Goulding, 1829).

The Shepherd's Calendar, 2 vols. (Edinburgh: Blackwood, and London: Cadell, 1829).

Songs, by the Ettrick Shepherd (Edinburgh: Blackwood, and London: Cadell, 1831).

A Queer Book (Edinburgh: Blackwood, and London: Cadell, 1832).

Altrive Tales: collected among the peasantry of Scotland, and from foreign adventurers, illustrated by George Cruikshank (London: Cochrane, 1832).

A Series of Lay Sermons on Good Principles and Good Breeding (London: Fraser, 1834).

Familiar Anecdotes of Sir Walter Scott (New York: Harper, 1834).

The Domestic Manners and Private Life of Sir Walter Scott (Glasgow: Reid, Edinburgh: Oliver and Boyd, and London: Black, 1834).

Tales of the Wars of Montrose, 3 vols. (London: Cochrane, 1835).

II Recent Editions of Works by James Hogg

Anecdotes of Sir W. Scott, edited, with an Introduction, by Douglas S. Mack (Edinburgh: Scottish Academic Press, 1983).

The Brownie of Bodsbeck, edited, with an Introduction, by Douglas S. Mack (Edinburgh and London: Scottish Academic Press, 1976).

Highland Tours, edited, with an Introduction, by William F. Laughlan (Hawick: Byway, 1981).

James Hogg: Selected Poems, edited, with an Introduction, by Douglas S. Mack (Oxford: Clarendon, 1970).

James Hogg: Selected Poems and Songs, edited, with an Introduction, by David Groves (Edinburgh: Scottish Academic Press, 1986).

James Hogg: Selected Stories and Sketches, edited, with an Introduction, by Douglas S. Mack (Edinburgh: Scottish Academic Press, 1982).

James Hogg: Tales of Love and Mystery, edited, with an Introduction, by David Groves (Edinburgh: Canongate, 1985).

Memoir of the Author's Life and Familiar Anecdotes of Sir Walter Scott, edited, with an Introduction, by Douglas S. Mack (Edinburgh and London: Scottish Academic Press, 1972).

The Private Memoirs and Confessions of a Justified Sinner, edited, with an Introduction, by Robert M. Adams (New York: Norton, 1970).

The Private Memoirs and Confessions of a Justified Sinner, edited, with an Introduction, by John Carey (London: Oxford Univ. Press, 1969).

The Private Memoirs and Confessions of a Justified Sinner, edited, with an Introduction, by John Wain (Middlesex: Penguin, 1983).

A Shepherd's Delight: A James Hogg Anthology, edited, with an Introduction, by Judy Steel (Edinburgh: Canongate, 1985).

The Three Perils of Man; War, Women and Witchcraft, edited, with an Introduction, by Douglas Gifford (Edinburgh and London: Scottish Academic Press, 1972).

III Some Works on James Hogg

CAMPBELL, Ian, 'Hogg's *Confessions* and the *Heart of Darkness*', *Studies in Scottish Literature*, XV (1980), 187-201.

DOUGLAS, Sir George, *James Hogg* (Edinburgh: Oliphant, 1899).

EGGENSCHWILER, David, 'James Hogg's *Confessions* and the Fall Into Division', *Studies in Scottish Literature*, July 1972, pp. 26-39.

GIFFORD, Douglas, *James Hogg* (Edinburgh: Ramsay Head, 1976).

GROVES, David, 'Allusions to *Dr Faustus* in James Hogg's *Justified Sinner*', *Studies in Scottish Literature*, XVIII (1983), 157-65.

GROVES, David, *James Hogg and the St. Ronan's Border Club* (Dollar: Mack, 1987).

GROVES, David, 'James Hogg, Burns, and "The Great W."', *Scottish Literary Journal*, Nov. 1985, pp. 19-22.

GROVES, David, 'Myth and Structure in James Hogg's *Three Perils of Woman*', *Wordsworth Circle*, Autumn 1982, pp. 203-10.

KIELY, Robert, *The Romantic Novel in England* (Cambridge, 1972).

MACK, Douglas, 'The Development of Hogg's Poetry', *Scottish Literary News*, Apr. 1973, pp. 1-8.

MACK, Douglas, 'Lights and Shadows of Scottish Life: James Hogg's *The Three Perils of Woman*', *Studies in Scottish Fiction: Nineteenth Century*, ed. Horst W. Drescher and Joachim Schwend (Frankfurt: Lang, 1985), pp. 15-27.

MACK, Douglas, 'The Devil's Pilgrim: a Note on Wringhim's Private Memoirs in James Hogg's *Confessions of a Justified Sinner*', *Scottish Literary Journal*, July 1975, pp. 36-39.

Newsletter of the James Hogg Society, ed. G. H. Hughes (1982 -).

PACHE, Walter, 'Der Ettrickschafer Hoggs: A Scotsman's Literary Reputation in Germany', *Studies in Scottish Literature*, Oct. 1970, pp. 109-17.

Papers given at the First Conference of the James Hogg Society, ed. Gillian H. Hughes (Stirling: James Hogg Society, 1984).

PARR, Norah, *James Hogg at Home: Being the Domestic Life and Letters of the Ettrick Shepherd* (Dollar: Mack, 1980). Highly recommended.

Scottish Literary Journal, Special James Hogg Number, ed. Thomas Crawford, May 1983.

SMITH, Nelson C., *James Hogg* (Boston: Twayne, 1980).

STROUT, Alan Lang, 'James Hogg's Forgotten Satire, *John Patterson's Mare*', *PMLA*, June 1937, pp. 427-60.

STROUT, Alan Lang, *The Life and Letters of James Hogg, the Ettrick Shepherd (1770-1825)* (Lubbock: Texas Tech, 1946). The unpublished second volume of this work resides in ms. in the National Library of Scotland.